The Ultimate
Women Associates'
Law Firm Marketing Checklist

The Renowned Step-by-Step,
Year-by-Year Checklist for Lawyers
Who Want to Develop Clients

Dedication

I wrote the first four-page version of this book 25 years ago when I was the marketing director of a large national law firm. I wanted to help the hard-working young lawyers who sought marketing support and based it upon my personal experience as a litigation associate and legal marketer.

A few years ago, I overhauled the material, turning it into a little book that people commended as offering useful, practical advice. Most marketing challenges lawyers confront do not vary by gender. But I understood that women lawyers often faced additional professional and client-development issues that their male peers did not. Which brings us to *this* book.

A friend suggested that I edit the book specifically to help young women lawyers navigate their way inside the firms. That sounded like an interesting idea but, obviously, I was not in the best position to credibly offer this advice. I *needed Susan Freeman*, CEO of Freeman Means Business.

A dynamic communications expert, Susan specializes in addressing the unique challenges women face inside law firms and other complex organizations. She helps women in business communicate effectively with the world—and helps men communicate with women in business. I wanted Susan's insight and candid, straight-talking style; I knew she'd offer a clear, real-world perspective. So, the marketing stuff is mine, but the gender context is all Susan.

Whether you're working inside a law firm, an organization or association, or hanging out your own shingle, Susan and I sincerely hope this book helps smooth out some of the bumps and gets you a little bit closer to achieving your dreams.

—Ross

Testimonials

"It is critical for women lawyers to have their own business and dictate their careers. This book details the plain-English steps to help women become successful business developers."

Sheila Murphy, Senior VP and Associate GC, MetLife

"I have long subscribed to the simple but powerful notion that "all good things begin with a list!" I can't think of a single tool that would be more valuable to an aspiring female associate striving to navigate her environs and successfully sow the seeds of personal investment in brand, career, and community, than the thoughtful and competent compass she'll find in the principles set forth by Susan and Ross."

Lisa Kremer Brown, Managing Director, Starbucks Law and Corporate Affairs

"Susan and Ross have created a comprehensive and actionable marketing checklist for young women lawyers. Most importantly, it is achievable. In fact, many of their principles would apply to any lawyer. It is quintessential reading for any female associate wanting to improve her personal brand or increase her business development."

Alan Bryan, Senior Associate General Counsel, Walmart

"I wish I'd known all this earlier in my career! And it's still a good reminder. This book is perfect for busy, overstretched junior lawyers. It offers pragmatic, realistic, and powerful advice in a concise, to-the-point format. Reading and following the authors' guidance will put associates at a real advantage compared to their peers. This is a book not just for associates but for anyone looking to take their career to the next level."

Nikki Stitt Sokol, Associate General Counsel, Facebook

"I wish I'd had the benefit of this guide to help me understand and navigate different

Testimonials

*conversational styles and marketing
best practices early in my career."*

Liam Brown, Founder and Executive Chairman, Elevate

*"This guide should be required reading for all associates who
want to have a successful career. Business development
is the most important skill a partner needs to have, and
this guide outlines an excellent—client-centered—way
to go about it. As a client, I would find the approach
described in this book to be highly effective."*

Susan Alker, COO and GC, Crescent Cove Capital Mgmt

*"If you're looking for a book that helps women lawyers
navigate their professional and marketing challenges, then
Susan and Ross are two authors who can share a solid
roadmap. From their years of legal expertise and marketing
creativity, they share how to build marketing infrastructure and
to communicate more effectively. They also offer guidance
regarding gender-based communication and demonstrate
the best ways to develop a personal brand. This is one big
marketing checklist, and if it's followed closely, will help readers
to build better relationships with their colleagues and clients."*

Deirdre Breakenridge, CEO, Pure Performance Communications

*The differences in gender communication cannot
be ignored! Lucky for us, Susan and Ross brilliantly
guide us in understanding the current climate and give
practical steps to be an effective communicator.*

Jennifer Turgeon, Manager Marketing and
BD, Hooper, Lundy & Bookman

*"This is an incredibly useful resource to get associates on track
towards productive, career-long, business development habits."*

Bettina Rutherford, Business Development Manager, K&L Gates

ADDITIONAL BOOKS BY ROSS FISHMAN

THE ULTIMATE LAW FIRM ASSOCIATE'S MARKETING CHECKLIST

*The Renowned Step-by-Step,
Year-by-Year Process for Lawyers
Who Want to Develop Clients*

WE'RE SMART. WE'RE OLD.
AND WE'RE THE BEST AT EVERYTHING.

*The World's First No-BS Guide to
Legal Marketing and Branding.*

THE ULTIMATE LAW FIRM ASSOCIATE'S MARKETING CHECKLIST
(CHINESE EDITION)

Edited by Cherry Zhang, LL.M.

THE ULTIMATE LAW STUDENT
GET-A-JOB CHECKLIST

Edited by Kerriann Stout, Esq.

THE ULTIMATE PUBLIC RELATIONS
HANDBOOK FOR LAWYERS

Co-Author, John Hellerman

Available at fishmanmarketing.com and amazon.com

THE ULTIMATE WOMEN ASSOCIATES'
LAW FIRM MARKETING CHECKLIST

**The Renowned Step-by-Step,
Year-by-Year Process for Lawyers
Who Want to Develop Clients**

By

Ross Fishman, JD
CEO, Fishman Marketing, Inc.

Susan Freeman, MA
CEO, Freeman Means Business

Published by Ross Fishman, Highland Park, Illinois
www.fishmanmarketing.com

ISBN: 9781095417539
Manufactured in the United States

Cover design by Michelle Benjamin

A Word on Gender Differences in Communication

Men and women speak differently. We communicate differently. We perceive the world differently. In general, this makes the world a more vibrant and interesting place. But it can also create confusion and misunderstanding. And that's what this book is intended to help address. We're going to focus on how those differences affect how women lawyers market and get promoted within law firms and organizations.

At its foundation, the academic discipline of communication focuses on how people use messages to generate meaning. We intuitively understand that there are countless different conversational styles that are shaped by, for example, where you grew up, your ethnic background, age, class, and gender. But style is invisible; we think that if we simply say what we mean then others will "get it."

Decades of research has proven that that's simply not true. And this disconnect can lead to misunderstanding, confusion, and frustration.

Throughout this book, we will offer guidance regarding gender-based communication. We recommend considering these lessons when building relationships with colleagues and clients. When you truly comprehend the language and style of your audience, you have a better chance of building meaningful relationships.

There are common conversational rituals within the genders, like men's joking put-downs, or women downplaying their authority. When everyone present is familiar with these conventions, they work just fine. But when a manner of speaking is not well understood, otherwise harmless comments might come across as unprofessional or offensive, creating workplace conflict that can damage relationships and careers.

Book Overview

Marketing's not difficult—plan, prepare, and execute steadily over time. A little bit every week. *Drip, drip, drip.* Just make sure the things you are doing are the *right* things.

That's what this book is designed to facilitate. Here's the plan:

- ❑ Engage in effective communication to build relationships that result in a higher profile and more clients.

- ❑ Learn to be a great lawyer, emphasizing keen technical skills, effective communication, and superior client service. Remember, when you're young, you can't just bring in the work, you've gotta be able to do it too.

- ❑ Build your long-term marketing infrastructure, the social-media platform and other tools you'll leverage through partnership and beyond.

- ❑ Join a local bar association, meet your peers, get active, and build your resume.

- ❑ Gradually add more external marketing and networking activities. Create a strong personal brand.

- ❑ Develop a narrow specialty or industry niche in an area you enjoy. Focus your marketing on a smaller trade group where you can get traction more quickly and leverage your relationship-building skills.

- ❑ Spend more time out of the office with prospects and referral sources as you gain more experience.

- ❑ Do what you love and love what you do!

That's the big picture; the rest of the book will detail the specific activities. If you have any questions, feel free to contact us:
susan@freemanmeansbusiness.com
ross@fishmanmarketing.com

We'd be delighted to hear from you.

Table of Contents

Preface

Ross's Preface

The law is a challenging, competitive profession; many associates live in a constant state of unease. They want to know how they're doing, how they're comparing to their peers in the firm and across the industry. And the anxiety doesn't disappear as they advance through their careers. In fact, it often increases, as they wonder if they're doing everything they can to improve their chance of promotion or autonomy, including developing their own clients.

I regularly see smart, personable, highly motivated senior associates or junior partners who have been working tirelessly on client development for many years with nothing to show for it. After we discuss their marketing efforts, it's often obvious to me that the activities they'd been undertaking had little chance of success. I don't want to discourage them, even when I'd like to say, "Yeah, that stuff was never going to work." It's not their fault; they just got bad advice. Or no advice at all.

I vividly remember my years as a litigation associate, receiving at most a few hours of marketing training per year. Eventually, I left the practice of law to market law firms full time, first as a big-firm Marketing Director, then Marketing Partner. There was always a steady stream of associates dropping by my office, hungry for practical, realistic advice and assistance. The guidance they'd received from their bosses and mentors, typically aging white men, tended toward "Here's what I did [i.e. 30 years ago, before the Internet]."

This continues today, with many firms wanting to conduct their marketing training using their senior partners. I've participated in hundreds of law firm marketing training programs and retreats, many of which included presentations by firm rainmakers, only a handful of whom actually offered useful advice. However well intentioned, it's difficult for many of these guys to deeply understand the different professional challenges women face at home and in today's workplace, and the conflicting communication styles between men and women.

Candidly, most of these rainmakers have no idea *how* they generated the business. They might think *they* know, but it's just their gut feeling. They know *something* worked, but only rarely what it really was. Further, a lot has changed since a 65-year-old set out to build his or her early practice. Back then, it was a seller's market for legal services. There were no global firms. No legal-outsourcing companies. No Internet or social media. You could hear the clacking of the typewriters.

It's hard to credibly offer networking advice to a 30-year-old lawyer when your LinkedIn profile has no text, one connection, and you don't know your password. Further, how useful is the advice of a gray-haired old guy whose wife stayed home with the kids to a 30-year-old working woman with small children?

Typical associate laments include:

- ❑ "I'm already billing 1,800 hours. I'm the primary caregiver at home, I don't have time to market."

- ❑ "What she *really* did was inherit a book of business from a retired partner."

- ❑ "[Joe Rainmaker] is charming, funny, and the life of the party; he's out drinking with prospects every night. I'm a young, single woman—his approach is never going to work for me."

- ❑ "She keeps saying, 'Good work is the best marketing.' What, our competitors aren't good lawyers too?"

So, without much guidance or an effective road map, associates' business-development activities tend toward occasional and opportunistic rather than proactive and strategic. Betting their future success on happenstance or providence won't cut it. "Hope" is not a strategy. They need a plan. A *realistic* plan.

Since opening Fishman Marketing 20+ years ago, I've conducted hundreds of firm retreats and marketing-training programs. I've seen the exact same nervousness in associates at nearly every single firm, from Illinois to Istanbul. From Ghana to Gary, Indiana.

Associates kept asking for a simple, practical, and detailed guide to follow—a step-by-step list of precisely what marketing and business-development activities to undertake to avoid floundering and increase the chance that they'll have their own business when they need it.

Susan and I have worked hard to keep the guide relevant, keeping up with the advancements in marketing technology and the lessons learned in gender-based and non-binary (those who don't identify as male or female) communication. Since the dawn of the digital age, much has changed in professional-services marketing, business development, and client service—especially for lawyers.

Women lawyers are pulled in many directions, some have said they feel like they're being pulled apart. So, this book advocates simplicity. When marketing time is precious, don't spend it spinning your wheels. We'll focus on the most efficient strategies and approaches. And along the way, we'll offer some gender-specific survival skills and communications advice that should help you work within male-dominated firms in a male-dominated profession. Women have long sought a simple guide to get the most out of their careers, without sacrificing unreasonably.

What follows is that guide.
—Ross

Susan's Preface
The Story of "Susie No More"

A professional man's wardrobe options are quite limited— basically dark suits, a blazer, pale shirts, plain pants. Curiously, this lack of choice is actually quite freeing. This forced uniformity prevents men from being labeled based upon their clothing choices. A professional woman has near-infinite options in clothing, hairstyle, and makeup. Every choice, every decision, leaves her vulnerable to being subtly criticized, categorized, and "marked."

When I worked in financial services in Boston, I started as a young "Southern Girl." Not too long into my time there, a helpful colleague volunteered to "reinvent" me. I was surprised by and curious about this suggestion. I said, "Sure." With that, she calmly proceeded to list the many things I needed to change about myself in order to be successful in this white man's world—the corporate world.

As I sat listening, I was mortified—but captivated. Apparently, to succeed, I would need to fit in better. Fitting in played into the "likability factor" that is so vital to a woman's success. The firm's culture was created by rich, white, northern men with whom I had little in common. But at the time, I was willing to reinvent myself for the sake of "success." Here are the top five suggestions my colleague made:

#1: No more "Susie," the name I had been called since childhood. I'd need to revert to the more formal "Susan," my birth name.

#2: No more big hair. I thought, "What is 'big hair' anyway?"

#3: No more bright colors. Well that was depressing. Off to Talbots for black, gray, navy, and brown pantsuits.

#4: No more "Please and thank you, sir. If you don't mind could you, would you, ma'am?"

#5: And lastly, absolutely no more excited high-pitched delivery. Apparently, I needed to lower my voice at least an octave.

To fit into the white man's corporate world, I would need to tone myself down.

In the study of communications, there is a tool called Muted Group Theory (MGT) that explains the dynamics of interactions between dominant or majority and sub-dominant or minority groups—such as men and women. White men created the system within which we currently operate. The language of the white male is the dominant language. Women and other minorities often struggle to navigate within the white-male corporate setting because of this. MGT explains the subtle and sometimes not-so-subtle overlapping power issues that exist at work. MGT states:

> *The language of a particular culture does not serve all its speakers equally, for not all speakers contribute in an equal fashion to its formulation. Women and other minorities are not as "heard" because the words and the norms have been formulated by the dominant group—white men.*

In our experience in training professionals in effective communication, we have found this revelation to be among the most important factors in creating change. Equity in the workplace starts by acknowledging that we all have different perspectives. No particular style is more valid than another but the differences can create conflict. It's like one person speaking Italian and another speaking French—both languages are legitimate but if you aren't fluent in both, effective communication doesn't take place.

It seems for all the success women have enjoyed in climbing that corporate ladder, they have often done so by copying the very men they fought so hard against in order to succeed; that needs to change.

Many millennials are throwing out the rule book and embracing their authentic selves in the workplace. I find that shift to be refreshing. Law firms have proven slow to adopt the "be me" culture, but things seem to be changing, supported by a younger generation of law firm leaders.

The best advice may be to *conform where you must and be yourself where you can*. As you advance in your career, you will find that the more power and influence you wield, the more you are free to be yourself.

I say, if you can, *"Find who you are—and be that"*!

—Susan

Introduction

As a new associate, your goal should not be to bring in work, but to master the skills you need to be an excellent lawyer and to put yourself in the best-possible position to successfully develop a pipeline of high-quality legal work *later*, when you will be expected to generate work or create business opportunities.

To do that, your goal from the very beginning of your associate career should be to build a strong and productive network. Gradually and systematically, over time, you will want to build a tight 250-500-person network of people who hire lawyers, influence the hiring decisions, or refer business to them. In order to do this, you must play to your strengths, become aware of the biases that women may face in the legal profession, and learn how to overcome them.

Few clients will hire an associate for a large case or deal; you simply don't offer enough cover if a representation were to go bad. ("Wait, you hired an *associate* for this?!") Therefore, spend these important early years building your resume, reputation, and name recognition within a significant, specific target audience.

Note: For busy professionals, the fastest, most-efficient path to having a sustainable, portable practice is to become one of the go-to experts in a small niche industry or sub-subset of a larger industry. Clients declare "industry expertise" to be among the traits they value most in their lawyers. Your goal shouldn't be "do more marketing" but rather to become a member of the "automatic short list" for some type of legal work within a finite audience of target clients.

For example, a woman friend of mine developed a $2 million/year book of sustainable business in her mid-30's just filing "small, Midwest-based, securities-industry, broker-dealer raiding lawsuits." (I discuss this niche strategy in greater detail below, under "A Plea to Focus Your Marketing.")

As an associate, focus on *helping people*, not looking for legal work. You want to be viewed as a knowledgeable, trusted insider, not a needy salesperson. Build a large number of close relationships following the steps below and you'll significantly increase the chance that you'll have your own clients when you need them. Fortunately, women often find that "form close relationships" is a more comfortable initial goal than "go get business."

In all your networking, remember, as a friend of mine once said, "It's better to be *interested* than to be *interesting*." Be more interested in them and in facilitating their success than being the life of the party or center of attention. Just because the stereotypic rainmakers are gregarious doesn't mean that's why they get hired. Their outgoing personality grows their network, but they get hired because they are good at listening and finding ways to help people solve their problems. And the studies show that women are better listeners than men. Use this as a strategic advantage.

As my father used to say, "When you're talking, you're not selling." When you are talking, you cannot possibly be learning. Listening and learning go hand-in-hand.

This book contains an extensive list of activities, but they're not intended to be exhaustive or mandatory. You needn't follow every single step. If you don't want to give speeches, for example, if that's not your thing, that's entirely OK. Maybe do a little more of some of the other things. Just be intentional, deliberate, and consistent over time. Look ahead. Have a plan. Work the plan. You'll be surprised how fast the years will pass, so start soon.

If you're in a big hurry, then compress the timeline. If you're starting your own practice or are at a smaller firm where you're expected to bring in clients right away, you have less time to develop your legal skills and marketplace reputation. You'll need to get out there, meet people, leverage existing relationships, and find that critical business or industry niche that will give you something credible to sell.

A landmark study by my friend Dr. Larry Richard ("Herding Cats: The Lawyer Personality Revealed") showed that lawyers are in the 13th percentile for being "sociable" compared to an average of 50th percentile for the general public. The good news is, although you might be quiet, shy, and hate marketing, most of your competitors are the same way. Don't beat yourself up, clients have pretty low social expectations for their lawyers.

Marketing's not hard. It's just hard *work*.

Turn the page and we'll start showing you how.

First-Year Associates

MINDSET:

Become an excellent lawyer.

Don't lose touch with the people you know.

Build a strong, professional marketing foundation.

Your first priority is to learn to be a great lawyer; external marketing isn't important yet. Your only real proactive activity should be ensuring that you don't lose touch with the people you already know. Be a pretty good connector and a really good communicator. If you belong to a women's group such as the National Association of Women Lawyers (NAWL) or Women-Owned Law (WOL), get involved in volunteer activities that cement relationships. You'll be quite busy, but it will be worth it.

Maintain relationships with friends from college and law school and any organizations you belong to. Create a reminder to make sure that you've had some contact with your gal-pals once per quarter. Your future self will thank you.

This is the year you should create the basic platform you'll be working from over the next few years. The infrastructure will gradually expand over time:

❑ Join one local, state, or national **bar association** and get involved in one targeted educational committee within your practice area.
  ○ Meet your peers.
  ○ Get to know businesswomen in other professional-services areas.
  ○ Learn your craft.
  ○ Invest in your profession.
  ○ Your long-term goal should be to chair a small committee during your fifth year of practice.

❑ Read your firm's website, internal website portal, newsletters, LinkedIn or Facebook pages, and other marketing materials to learn about your firm's range of services and clients.
  ○ Read your senior associates' and partners' biographies and profiles as well, to learn about their practices and outside interests. This will come in handy later.

❑ Build your personal brand within your law firm.
  ○ Focus on internal marketing by developing relationships with your firm's lawyers, both inside and outside of your practice area.
  ○ Also focus on getting to know the professional staff at your firm, they will be able to serve as a sounding board and guide to internal relationships.

❑ Do not spend your career eating lunch at your desk. Go out at least:
  ○ Once each week with a firm lawyer inside your practice area

- ○ Twice each month with a firm lawyer outside of your practice area
- ○ Regularly with friends and contacts

❑ Be authentic in both your verbal and nonverbal communication.
- ○ Dress in a manner that communicates your own personal and professional style.

🗨 The many choices a professional woman faces in her clothing, hairstyle, and makeup leave her vulnerable to being stereotyped in ways that may hinder her career.

The safer option may be to tone down your fashion choices early in your career, to help fit in and avoid prejudice by any narrow-minded partners. As you attain more autonomy and success, you may choose to expand your look to better express your personal style.

❑ Monitor your office visitor list.
- ○ Stop by and introduce yourself to the lawyers visiting from other offices.
- ○ If there is time and it's appropriate, ask to grab a coffee.

❑ Draft a detailed website biography, following the firm's format.
- ○ Update it regularly, especially when your practice is developing.
- ○ Ideally, you should update it every time a matter you are involved with concludes, you publish an article or give a presentation, are appointed to a committee, etc.
- ○ Make it a habit that when you update your biography you also update the matters you have worked on in your firm's experience-management or knowledge-management system, such as Foundation.
- ○ Update it thoroughly at least every six months.
- ○ Be judicious in what you include.
  - • Delete all items from high school.
  - • Be sensible regarding college activities.
- ○ Delete any *Who's Who* directory "honors" or other questionable accolades. See the blog post at *http://goo.gl/jWrQIY*.

❑ Build your network. Create a mailing list of friends and contacts. Don't forget to leverage your firm's Client Relationship Management (CRM) system; you never know where your classmates will end up. By participating in your firm's CRM program, you can leverage your relationships to help create introductions with various technology tools your firm may use, such as RelSci. There are several easy-to-use CRM platforms on the market and if that's not doable, use a basic Excel spreadsheet.

❑ Opt for more, rather than fewer people, when deciding whom to add.
  ○ Law school classmates
  ○ Childhood, high school, and college friends
  ○ Former colleagues
  ○ Community association and professional club contacts
  ○ Parents of your children's friends, and contacts made through your children's activities

❑ Keep in touch with your existing network, leveraging both traditional and online tools, like:
  ○ Events, newsletters, holiday cards, breakfasts, lunches, drinks, phone calls
  ○ Social media, e.g., LinkedIn, Facebook, Twitter, etc.

❑ Before you engage in any marketing or social media, review
  ○ Your firm's social media policy
  ○ Your state's ethics rules governing the use of marketing, communication, and social media (generally Rules 7.1–7.4, see *http://goo.gl/JOhhF*)

There are nearly 600 million people using **LinkedIn** every day for networking; it is the most important social media tool for young professionals, the one preferred by lawyers. It hasn't quite taken off as a communication platform, but it's the foundation of most professionals' personal marketing. It's where you'll post articles and updates, and connect to your growing network.

Today, nearly everyone you would want to hire you in any capacity will first skim your LinkedIn profile to learn more about you. Make it persuasive and professional. Show them that you're more than a dispassionate one-page resume. This is your opportunity to help your targets see how wonderful you are.

❑ If you don't have a LinkedIn page, create one.
  ○ Be sure to establish your purpose and personalize your page.

- ○ Draft a detailed LinkedIn personal profile.
- ○ Infuse it with your vibrant personality.
- ○ Ensure there are no typos. Zero. None.

❑ Fill it out completely, including the Contact Information and Education sections.
- ○ Fill it out completely, including the Summary, Contact Information, Experience, and Education sections.
- ○ The two most-important areas are Summary and Experience.
  - The Summary section is the very first thing people will read after your name and headline.
  - The Experience section is where you get the opportunity to highlight all the exciting ways you have built up your personal brand and specialty niche (that will be covered below under "A Plea to Focus Your Marketing").
- ○ Read "Drafting a Persuasive LinkedIn Profile" in the Addendum.

❑ Build a sizable LinkedIn network, work toward hundreds of connections.
- ○ Start by connecting with people you know personally such as family, friends, peers, acquaintances, and classmates from all your schools.
- ○ Your goal is to get to "500+" connections as soon as possible. Once you hit 500 connections, LinkedIn just shows "500+" on your profile. This works as social proof to others that you have an established professional network.
  - Join your law school LinkedIn group, and connect with anyone you know.
  - Consider starting a group for your law school graduation class.
- ○ Join your firm's LinkedIn group.
- ○ Once you have a complete profile and established network you can start reaching out to additional people whom you'd like to connect with such as professors, speakers you've heard at events, individuals who work at firms you are interested in, etc.

❑ Add a quality photograph.
- ○ This single head shot encapsulates your entire professional image. Be smart.
  - No cropped vacation, party, or wedding or group photos.
  - Nothing cute, grainy, badly lit, or blurry.
  - No pets or props.
- ○ An inexpensive passport photo from Walgreens will suffice.
- ○ You should dress similar to how you would look at a professional event. Smile.

- ❑ If you have an existing LinkedIn page, do a thorough audit to ensure it is highly professional.
  - ○ Sanitize it so there's nothing a 65-year-old client or the most conservative senior partner would find offensive.
  - ○ Be judicious in what you include.
    - • Delete all items from high school.
    - • Be sensible regarding college activities.
  - ○ Write in the first person and use a friendly, casual tone.
  - ○ Create a custom public profile URL, so it's not random letters and numbers. Find an explainer video online that details the simple steps.
  - ○ Review the privacy settings for your profile. You want your profile to be set to "Public" so that people can see and connect with you. However, it is important to keep in mind that anything you "like" or "comment" on will be visible to anyone in your network, so use discretion.
  - ○ Post occasional relevant updates, including thought-leadership pieces you have written in your chosen area of specialization/focus.
    - • It's easy to start by sharing or liking things that others in your specialty area have posted.
  - ○ Remember, listening and engaging with what others post is as important in social networking as what you say and post.
  - ○ No one expects your profile to be very long; just write simply and proficiently.
  - ○ Update it regularly, at least every few months, especially when your career is developing.
  - ○ Ideally you should update it every time you publish an article, give a presentation, are on a new committee, etc.
  - ○ Check it at least weekly.

- ❑ Regularly "Endorse" classmates, friends, and peers; it only takes a click. They'll typically endorse you back. Create evidence that you are well-liked, a leader among your group.
  - ○ A word of caution with Skills and Endorsements: When you receive an endorsement from someone for a specific skill, only post it on your bio if you have actual expertise in that area. Some state bar rules have restrictions on this.
  - ○ When in doubt, leave it off.

- ❑ Note when your network changes jobs or celebrates a birthday or work anniversary.
  - ○ Use that as a personal opportunity to connect and congratulate them.

- ○ Anyone whose LinkedIn profile you visit will receive a notification that you'd been there.
- ○ You can turn this off and browse in Stealth Mode. There are simple explainer videos on this topic. Find one and watch it.

❑ If you don't have LinkedIn's Sales Navigator, get it.
- ○ Who do you know who I'd want to know? TeamLink Extend is a LinkedIn feature that allows you to see the connections of up to 1,000 of your colleagues, alumni, or board members.

❑ Daily News Feed. Your existing LinkedIn feed provides updates regarding your friends, colleagues, law school classmates, et al., like a Facebook version of your LinkedIn page. You can create "professional" versions of your LinkedIn page via Navigator.
- ○ Rather than sending connection requests to prospects, use LinkedIn's "Save Account/ Save Lead" button. By saving, you're tracking the posts of your target accounts and anyone that you'd like to follow within those accounts, without having to reach out to those individuals directly.

Twitter is a simple, efficient platform to connect yourself to your specialty area online. Permitting just 280 characters—a couple casual sentences and hashtags—it is an ideal communications platform to help build your brand and connect with others in a specialty area or industry niche.

❑ If you don't have a **Twitter** account, create one under your name.
- ○ For example, Ross is @*rossfishman* and Susan Freeman is @ *susfree*.
- ○ Check it occasionally.

❑ Build your Twitter network; connect with your peers, professors, industry contacts, and thought leaders.
- ○ Follow people, companies, associations, and organizations within your legal, business, and specialty niche areas of interest.

❑ Post weekly on something relating to your chosen specialty area.
- ○ Remember to include the narrow search engine optimized (SEO) keywords that the media and experts in this industry or area would use to search.
- ○ Ensure you learn the nuances of the jargon.

❏ Re-tweet the tweets that resonate with you, to help grow your network.

❏ Consider utilizing Twitter as a listening platform to better understand your specialty area, scholars, and more.
  ○ Pay attention to what they are promoting, discussing, and commenting on. It can all be valuable.

facebook

❏ If you don't have a Facebook page, create one.
  ○ If you do have a Facebook page from college, law school, etc., conduct a thorough audit to ensure it is now professional.
  ○ Update your security settings.
  ○ Hide the party photos, etc.
  ○ Sanitize it so there's nothing a 65-year-old client or the most conservative senior partner would find offensive.
  ○ Keep it casual and sensible.
  ○ Check it at least weekly, from home.
  ○ Join your law school alumni Facebook group.
  ○ Connect with your friends, especially those from law school.

❏ Sign up for Google Alerts at *www.google.com/alerts*. See video at *https://goo.gl/bAeQhj*.
  ○ Put the Search Terms in quotes so the words will be searched together.
    • Two important searches include "[your name]" and "[your firm's name]."
  ○ Consider also creating alerts on friends and prospects.
    • Drop them a quick email when you see them mentioned.
    • Even more powerful is a short, handwritten note.
  ○ Reach out to your firm's library and knowledge-management professionals to identify other alerts and news feeds you may want to subscribe to.

Client Service

❏ Develop a reputation for providing the highest-quality client service.
  ○ Remember, the profession is full of smart, technically skilled lawyers.

- The lawyers whom clients value most are those who excel at communication, timeliness, accessibility, and likeability.
- Keep clients regularly informed regarding the current status of their matters.
  - Send them copies of all relevant correspondence.
- Always call clients back promptly, ideally within two hours.
  - Consider: if you have a sick child, how would you feel about a pediatrician who has an "All calls returned within 24 hours" policy?
  - If you are unavailable (e.g. on a plane, in court, etc.), have your secretary or assistant check your phone messages regularly.
    - Have them return the call.
    - Explain that you will be unavailable until a particular time.
    - Ask if they would like their call returned at that time, or if they would prefer having someone else address the issue sooner.
- Give clients and prospects your cell number.
  - They will appreciate the offer and won't abuse the privilege with late-night or weekend calls.
  - Consumer clients (e.g. divorce and criminal defense) are the exception. They will call. You may not want to give them your number.
  - Check your email at least once every night and daily on weekends.

Business cards

- ❑ Always, always, always have business cards with you; you never know when you're going to meet someone who could later turn into a client or referral source.
  - The box of 250 cards gathering dust in your desk drawer can't help you unless they're with you when you need them.
  - Leave 75–100 in the box at work, then divide up the rest among your purses, briefcase, backpack, suitcase, glove box, pants pockets, suit coats, blazers, jackets, overcoats, gym bags, etc.
  - Put a thick stack in your suitcase, so you don't forget them when traveling.
  - Women's outfits may not have pockets that help keep cards easily accessible.
    - Plan for networking events by wearing a blazer with pockets.
    - Bring a purse with a shoulder strap. Keep your cards in an

outside pocket so you can effortlessly pull them out with one hand.
- You may be able to hold a few in the back of your conference name badge.
- At networking events, to avoid embarrassing mix-ups, always keep your own cards in your left-side pockets, and the cards you collect on your right side.
- Watch the video at *https://youtu.be/rAA3291QWnQ*.

❑ The goal is not to simply pass out cards to attendees.
- You must collect their cards as well, to ensure that you can manage the flow of communications and effectively follow up with them.
- Do not put the burden on them to stay in touch.
- Read more under "Networking and Attending Seminars" below.

❑ If you're starting your own firm:
- Find a way to connect with a senior lawyer—a mentor who can offer guidance, help teach you some skills, and throw you some overflow work.
- Your first clients will be your previous relationships.
- There are many practical new resources dedicated to this area online. Also:
  - Consider joining the ABA's GPSolo group, *www.americanbar. org/groups/gpsolo*
  - Buy Jay Foonberg's "How to Start and Build a Law Practice."

Second-Year Associates

MINDSET:

Build your internal brand and develop your network.

Your first priority as a second-year associate remains learning to be a great lawyer; marketing is still a distant second.

Continue to focus on building your internal brand for excellence, efficiency, and teamwork.

❑ Continue the "First-Year Associates" activities, above.

❑ Stay in touch with your friends and contacts.

❑ Continue adding new names to your mailing list and to your LinkedIn and Facebook networks as you encounter these contacts.

- ○ Bar association committee members
- ○ Your peers within client companies
- ○ People you meet at networking functions
- ○ Alumni association contacts
- ○ Co-counsel and opposing counsel

❑ Join LinkedIn groups of the associations and industries you are involved in.
- ○ Pay attention to the conversations, noting the gender-based differences in online communication style, including how men and women may vary in choice of words, use of emojis, apologies, and compliments.

❑ Continue improving your technical skills by attending local seminars and reading bar association and legal profession trade magazines and law-specific blogs and online news sources.

❑ Volunteer for firm committees and activities when lawyer help is needed.
- ○ It's a great way to raise your profile and get to know people in other areas of the firm.
- ○ Also begin to volunteer to help with practice group activities such as drafting matters for rankings and awards such as Chambers or Legal 500.

❑ Volunteer to help firm lawyers or business-development professionals compile client pitches and presentations, to gain an understanding of the process.

Third-Year Associates

MINDSET:

Continue developing your external network, including relationships with your in-house contemporaries.

Start developing a toolkit of the soft skills that will become increasingly important to your success, e.g., an elevator speech, public speaking, writing or co-authoring articles or blog posts, and interpersonal communication skills to inspire confidence.

By now you're getting a better handle on your legal practice. Continue improving your technical skills, but you can begin to be more proactive in growing your network.

❑ Continue the First- and Second-Year Associates activities, above.

❑ Build your resume by participating more actively in your bar association within your practice area.
  ○ Volunteer for a committee and work toward a leadership position.
  ○ Write a brief article for a committee newsletter, they're always looking for content to publish.
  ○ Give a speech on an area of particular interest. If you're uncomfortable presenting solo to a group, start by speaking on a panel or with a co-presenter.

❑ Increase your marketing efforts; devote time each week to a proactive networking activity, e.g., meals, sports, professional events, etc.

   🔊 This is the point where many women with young families at home struggle with work-life balance. Do not engage in or accept indiscriminate, non-strategic, or one-off initiatives—what some call "random acts of lunch."

   When your time is precious, you must ensure that your efforts are synergistic and focused on a specific and achievable goal. Read the "A Plea to Focus Your Marketing" chapter below.

❑ Master a basic "elevator speech" (plenty of good explainer videos are available online).
  ○ Tell people what you do in a memorable, personal way.
    • Tailor it to the unique needs of each specific audience or person.
    • Avoid using jargon.
    • Talk about the benefits of what you do.
    • Become known for something unique—a small niche.
    • Keep it so simple that a child could understand it.
      ○ Using unnecessarily large or obscure words can be considered pretentious.
    • See the video on this topic at *https://youtu.be/SH4mjyvXZEI*.
  ○ In addition to your elevator pitch, have short answers ready to everyday questions such as "How are you?"
    • Instead of proudly responding "Busy!" or "Swamped!" (which sounds negative), have an anecdote ready about a new matter you are working on or a new restaurant in town that you went to.

- Always remain upbeat, no one wants to hire (or work with) a complainer.

🗨 Be careful about communicating with deferential body language, as this can signal submissiveness. This includes standing off balance, crossing your arms and legs, or otherwise taking up less space.

Instead, to be perceived as confident, assume a more-expansive posture. Act like you belong there. When sitting in meetings, keep your torso upright or lean slightly forward. Uncross your arms and place them on the table. Men learn this as boys in the schoolyard. Women need to consciously undertake this behavior until it becomes effortless.

❑ Learn to turn social contacts into potential business contacts.
  ○ This is a long-term process; it takes typically at least 7 to 20 touch points with a new contact before you begin to have a chance of getting hired.
  ○ "Active listening" is important. Remember, this is where women have a particular advantage over their male competitors. Use it.
  ○ Come prepared to ask well-informed questions about their business.
    - Spend a few minutes conducting online research before you go to a lunch meeting.
    - Don't forget to leverage your firm's competitive-intelligence and knowledge-management tools.
  ○ Listen for opportunities to help them achieve their goals.
  ○ Find ways to help them become successful in their careers.
  ○ Ask your marketing professionals to bring in a networking-training program.
    - Networking is a learned skill. It's not difficult, but many behaviors are counterintuitive to most lawyers.
    - Most importantly, remember that work is brought in by listening, not talking.
  ○ Check your local bar association for marketing seminars.
  ○ See the brief video at *https://goo.gl/Bwq9ii*.

❑ Attend Communication Skills training offered by the firm.
  ○ If the firm doesn't offer it, request it. Firm management will be more likely to take this request seriously if a group of women associates request this training together.
  ○ Ensure it includes both general and gender-based and non-binary communication skills.

- Internal firm problems are more often caused by ignorance than malice.
- Educating firm leaders can expedite positive change inside your firm.
- Ask to make the training mandatory and seek CLE credit for it.

❑ Attend Marketing training offered by the firm.
   ○ If the firm doesn't offer it, request it.
   ○ Leading law firms are spending time and effort on both visibility-enhancing Marketing efforts as well as Business-Development (BD) activities.
      - BD is "sales," i.e. the activities traditionally undertaken by rainmakers bringing in the business.
   ○ See the video at https://goo.gl/4RxHNp.

❑ Look for opportunities to "cross-sell," i.e. diversify the work the firm receives from existing clients into a new practice area.
   ○ Associates often find that they're interacting with client personnel more frequently than the client-relationship partner. Use your phone calls and emails to develop a strong relationship with your peer inside the client company.
      - Be more than a cold, objective lawyer; where possible, become their friend.
   ○ When chatting with your peers inside client companies, casually inquire about their day, their job, the company and its inner workings (but never bill them for this time!).
   ○ Listen for new areas where they might need a lawyer. For example, did they mention that they were:
      - Having trouble with an employee? They might need an employment lawyer.
      - Considering buying a new building, expanding into a new state, or developing a new product or service? If so, mention these issues to the partner in charge of the client relationship.
   ○ Your goal is to make them think of you as the best, most caring and service-oriented lawyer they know. This helps solidify the firm's relationship with this client.
      - If your contact leaves and joins a different company, continue to stay in touch. You want them to call you when they need a lawyer.
      - If you receive that call, this new company becomes your client!

○ Follow your target clients' competitors to develop industry intelligence and gain insight by asking your peers thought-provoking questions about what their competitors are doing.

❑ Read legal and targeted industry publications, print and online.
  ○ Subscribe to blogs and follow Twitter accounts of leaders in these industries.

❑ Add select client and prospect names to your Google Alerts (e.g., "Fishman Marketing")
  ○ Use information you receive as a reason to contact, congratulate, or reconnect.

❑ Reach out to new lateral attorneys who join your firm.
  ○ Introduce yourself.
  ○ Develop relationships and become a helpful resource.

❑ Get to know your firm's marketing and business-development professionals.
  ○ They can be a great resource for you.
  ○ They often have valuable marketing opportunities to share. If they see that you respect them as professionals and value their advice and contributions, they're more likely to offer you the strategic perks that come across their desks.

❑ Update your LinkedIn profile.
  ○ Add organizations, volunteering experience, and honors and awards.
  ○ Add your top thought-leadership pieces to the Publications section and include a summary and the article URL.

🔍 Avoid "office housework." Women lawyers may subtly be assigned a disproportionate amount of the non-legal support tasks like taking the meeting notes, ordering or cleaning up lunch, planning meetings or parties, and printing documents.

This may include time-consuming but undervalued work such as organizing conferences or planning for summer interns. It is important to be seen as helpful, but not submissive. Managing Partners can pour the coffee without diminishing their status; young women fighting for professional credibility can't.

Solution: Rotate the office housework and use "The Strategic No." If you're asked to undertake Office Housework, do it once graciously, then work behind the scenes to ensure the task is rotated among your coworkers so you're not asked to do it again. As a way to avoid undervalued work, seek out career-enhancing assignments, such as managing a high-profile project.

Filling your plate with high-value work empowers you to turn down undervalued work. For example, you might say, "I'd love to help, but I'm working with Ted on an important strategic initiative. Bob would be perfect for this." If certain Housework tasks are unavoidable, bring an assistant to handle these responsibilities for you.

Fourth- and Fifth-Year Associates

MINDSET:

Continue refining your legal skills.

Expand your network and build your external reputation and resume.

Focus on client-service skills and interacting with clients.

Big-firm associates may transition to Senior Associate status.

Solos and small firm associates should be gaining traction.

A Plea to Focus Your Marketing

Around your fourth or fifth year, you should start focusing your marketing efforts more narrowly, particularly toward an industry group or sub-specialty practice niche. See the videos at *https://goo.gl/fKR7AA* and *https://goo.gl/QtmJTT*.

Here's the larger point: When the next recession hits, I wouldn't want to be just another smart and skilled but generic and easily replaced generalist. I'd rather be the one who offers more, a skill or expertise that your firm can't find in precisely the same quantity in every other associate in your class.

You also become much easier for others to cross-sell if you have a unique expertise that the partners can remember when in conversations with prospects. "You manufacture bicycles? [Or build prisons, or license offshore oil-rig technology, or...?] One of our corporate associates has expertise in that area!"

For new grads who are starting their own practice, it'll be some time before clients will seek you out purely for your legal talent. But if you're the lawyer who knows their industry best, you'll have an advantage over those who may have superior legal skills, but don't have your business insight. The fastest way for a newer lawyer to gain client-development traction is to find that specialty niche. Examples include being the "Philadelphia #MeToo Litigator" or the "Nevada Microbrewery Lawyer."

For example, I probably know more about Industrial Tire Manufacturing than just about any lawyer in the world—it's my family business. My father and grandfather designed and built tires for heavy equipment, like underground mining crawlers, loaders, etc. Growing up, the specs of new tire sizes and the composition of tire fill was typical dinner conversation. As a child, I played with toy forklifts and vulcanized rubber for my fifth-grade science-fair project. I worked summers in the sooty factory in high school—sneezing oily carbon-black out of my sinuses for weeks afterwards. I've flown in the Goodyear blimp. My sisters know this stuff too.

That is to say, I take for granted an insider's nuanced understanding of this narrow little billion-dollar industry. But practicing as a litigation associate, it never occurred to me that some group of clients would have found that unique knowledge to be valuable.

Instead of marketing "general commercial litigation to Chicago-area businesses" like countless other generic lawyers, I should have been marketing my tire-industry expertise to companies like Goodyear, John Deere, Caterpillar, the rubber importers, and chemical manufacturers.

They would have valued having a lawyer who knew their industry as well as they did. But it simply never occurred to me that I possessed any uniquely useful information. Now I know better.

It's not enough to specialize in the obvious industry sectors like real estate, health care, construction, financial services, or insurance—they are simply too broad. You must be more precise and find a niche within them (e.g., FCA litigator in health care, D&O liability in insurance). You will also find opportunities in smaller, more-defined and obscure areas where you have existing experience, interest, or contacts.

Think in terms of focusing on Pest Control rather than Banking. Not general Transportation Law but Transportation of Infectious Biological Material. See the video at: https://goo.gl/3GWNQa.

Consider segmenting it further by geography and/or the particular type of company or size of matter. The answer might not be obvious now; just look for it and recognize it when it comes along. It takes at least 2-3 years to build this, so start being proactive in this regard beginning around your fourth year.

For example, at Fishman Marketing we have developed marketing initiatives supporting lawyers and firms who targeted niche industries or practices including these:

- Ad valorem property tax cases in Chicago
- Alabama pest-control companies
- Backyard-barbecue propane tank explosions in Colorado
- Boy Scout-abuse personal injury cases in Chicago
- Bridge-and-tunnel construction companies in Florida
- College-athletics coaches in the SEC
- Cuban personal injury cases in South Florida
- Defending the Chicago police in Taser-related cases
- Divorce cases for Iranian immigrants living in Canada
- Ghanaian law firm seeking inbound referrals
- Global aircraft and railcar finance under U.S. law
- Health care lobbying and intellectual property
- Health care software licensing contracts
- Multi-generational family businesses
- New York companies doing business in Israel
- Northern California agriculture industry
- Oil and gas companies in Louisiana
- Personal injury cases for St. Louis Catholics
- Trucker DUI defense in northern British Columbia
- Upstate New York forestry and timber industry

Considerations in identifying the area to target include:

- Did you grow up in a family business?
- What was your college major?
- What hobby, passion, or special skill or interest of yours would clients value?
- What job did you have before law school?
- What's hanging on your walls or sitting on your coffee table?
- Where do you or your spouse have an established network?
- What do you know that other lawyers don't that would benefit some category of clients?
- What type of law do you practice? What are you seeing as growth trends within your practice?
- Think through your list of friends and family members. Are several of them in one particular industry or niche?
- Fill out one of the handy "Niche and Industry Marketing Checklists" in the Addendum.

To help you identify your narrow niche, visit a public or law library to review a printed copy of Gale Publishing's multi-volume Encyclopedia of Associations.

❑ Browse through the easy-to-use 25,000-association directory to identify the best trade groups or professional associations serving your target industry.

❑ Seek a 500 to 1,000-member national association with an active local chapter.
  ○ Call them to learn more about their members.
  ○ If the membership includes legal-hiring decision makers, consider joining the group.
  ○ Don't worry if the members are junior or mid-level professionals; build relationships with them when you're both starting your careers. They'll be able to start choosing their own lawyers when you're in a position to get hired.
  ○ Validate that group with your contacts who know it.

Once you have selected the organization or association, your ultimate goal is to become one of the "usual suspects" in that group—a highly visible, friendly, helpful, active contributor. This is basic target marketing. Your goal is to be a relatively big fish in a small, finite, industry pond. Spend a couple years just learning about the industry and the association members.

❑ Attend at least 8 out of 12 monthly local chapter meetings per year.

❑ Network regularly and actively; get to know everyone.

❑ Keep the conversations focused on them.
  ○ Remember the 80/20 Rule of Communication. You should spend just 20% of the time talking, mostly asking interested, insightful questions about them and their businesses, and 80% of the time listening.
    • Remarkably, studies show that the more they talk, (1) the smarter they think you are, and (2) the more they like you!
  ○ Be genuinely interested in them.

❑ Be helpful; offer advice and assistance.

❑ Become a frequent public speaker panelist or moderator.

❑ Join a committee and follow through on any assignments or responsibilities.
  ○ People will judge your legal skills based upon how you perform as a volunteer.
  ○ Do you meet your deadlines and commitments?

❑ Do not actively seek work or sell your firm, or you will be shunned as a <shudder> "vendor."

❑ Create a comfortable and safe space in which they want to partner with you.

❑ Try to understand "why they buy" not "how to sell to them."

When I got started in marketing, our profession's organization was the national Legal Marketing Association, with 300 members. Working in-house as a large firm's Marketing Manager, I was one of the few lawyers in the group. I discovered that I had something to contribute, that my knowledge of the law was helpful, so I began writing some articles for the local chapter and giving some speeches. They were well received, and I began to be invited to write and speak nationally. I was surprised to discover that I enjoyed it.

Within a few years, I realized that without even trying, I knew almost everyone in the entire national association. More importantly, they knew me as a helpful, trusted member of the legal marketing community. I'd dedicated my external communications activities toward a relatively small and finite group, just 300 people—half the size of my high school graduating class.

Over time, I just kept writing and speaking and networking. Writing and speaking and networking. Writing and speaking and networking. I later was invited to become the LMA's vice president, which further increased my visibility. None of this was especially complicated or challenging; it was just the basic blocking and tackling that anyone can do.

Eight years later, when I left the law firm to go into consulting and needed to get hired by law firms, the LMA had grown to 3,500 members, and I found that I knew most of them, or at least they'd frequently read my articles and seen me speak. I had a national network of thousands of prospects who knew what I did and had a generally positive impression of me and my expertise. I'd built this network entirely inadvertently. And with some basic planning and regular execution, absolutely anyone can do this intentionally and strategically.

For busy professionals trying to "have it all," targeting a small group or association is the single most-efficient strategy. When focused on a particular industry association, all of your marketing activities work synergistically together; no effort is wasted. When you write an article, they all read it. When you give a speech, they all watch it. When you do your networking, it's with the same audience that read your article and saw your speech. Everything you do builds upon everything you've done.

More for Fourth- and Fifth-Year Associates

Remember that providing the highest-quality technical skills and extremely responsive client service are essential elements of your firm's marketing to its existing clients.

As a fifth-year, you should chair a local bar association committee as a persuasive resume builder. You may also seek to create a new one, to leapfrog the competition. Finding that I enjoyed marketing, I called the American Bar Association to join the national Marketing Legal Services Committee. Sadly, I learned that it was defunct. I immediately offered to resurrect it if I could be the Chair. With nothing to lose, they happily agreed. It looked great on my nascent marketing resume.

❑ Identify a marketing mentor, ideally a young rainmaker who's invested in your future and can help answer questions and provide guidance and support.

❑ Form a posse. According to Joan Williams, Ph.D., women should organize a group of coworkers who will celebrate one another's successes.
  ○ You'll all benefit from this arrangement: promoting your coworkers is good for their careers and elevates your own status.

❑ Identify a male lawyer as an internal firm mentor, ideally a partner who's invested in your future and can help answer questions and provide guidance and support.
  ○ People like those who are most like them, meaning men are drawn to other men. As a result, women tend to receive less of the vital mentorship that accelerates careers—and are less likely to have a sponsor who advocates and opens doors for them. You may need to proactively seek one out.
  ○ Your firm mentor should provide input regarding how you can advance, putting your name forward for stretch assignments and promotions. He should meet you for lunch—and encourage other male partners to do the same for other women in the firm.

❑ Learn about your clients' and prospects' companies and industries.
  ○ Regularly read industry websites, publications, and blogs.
  ○ Conduct online research periodically to stay current on their issues and needs.
  ○ Browse company websites regularly, especially new-information areas like "About Us," "What's New," and "Press Releases."
  ○ Follow them on social media.
  ○ If your firm has a Competitive Intelligence team, work with them

to leverage firm tools like Manzama Insights to learn more about your target companies and decision makers.
- ○ Create a Google Alert for each company and important decision maker.

❑ Update significant matters you have worked on in your experience-management or knowledge-management system.
- ○ Also work with your marketing and business development professionals to learn about the key details that help matters stand out in rankings, awards, and Requests for Proposals (RFPs) and include that information in your write-ups.
- ○ These activities will help raise your profile with others in the firm who might not have had the chance to work with you yet.
- ○ See "How to Write Persuasive Case Summaries" in the Addendum.

❑ Notify your firm's marketers of significant cases and/or transactions you are involved in or aware of, for media and public relations purposes.

❑ Write a recurring column for targeted industry publications, print and online.

❑ Tweet at least weekly on issues relevant to your narrow area(s) of interest.

❑ Write an article for a legal or industry publication or blog on new issues, trends, or precedents relevant to your area(s) of interest.
- ○ Ask to include your head shot(s), which will enhance your networking and brand.
- ○ Invite a client to co-author it with you, as a nice value-add.
  - • Most likely, you'll do 90% of the work.
  - • Frame a reprint and give it to the client over a follow-up lunch. It'll hang on their office wall, with your face on it.
- ○ Another option is to use the article as an opportunity to get a meeting with a valuable prospect.
  - • "I'm writing an article on XYZ and I need to quote an expert on this topic. Could I interview you for the article next week over lunch?"
    - ○ This is a great way to meet important executives.
  - • This is just the first contact. Remember, it could take a dozen more before they would potentially be willing to send you some business.
    - ○ It's a marathon, not a sprint.

❑ Give a presentation to a legal, industry, or community association or at an in-house client seminar. Carefully select the topic, using it to support your chosen niche or specialty practice.
  ○ If you enjoy speaking, seek to build a reputation as a strong presenter; there aren't many lawyers who can be both substantive and entertaining.
  ○ Your goal should not be to simply give a nice, educational speech—it's to give the speech that the audience will remember next week.
    • Raise the bar and strive to give the best darn speech at the entire conference, the one every attendee will be talking about.
  ○ Great presenters build their reputation quickly.
    • Even if yours isn't the best speech, the attempt will improve the quality significantly.
    • You're likely to get invited back next year and word will spread around the industry.
  ○ Audiotape and transcribe the speech or use voice-to-text software.
    • This single transcribed speech can be repurposed into dozens of different-length articles and blog posts for various audiences.
    • Edit the transcription into dozens of tweets and social media updates.
    • Professional editors can do much of this work for you, if you have a marketing budget.
      ○ "Here's the 10,000-word transcription of my speech. Please edit this into 100 tweets, 10 blog posts, one 5,000-word article, three 1,250-word articles, and five 500-word articles."
    • Get professional presentation training. Public speaking is a learned skill.
    • Rehearse, rehearse, rehearse.
    • Ensure you get videotaped and review it afterward.
      ○ It can be mortifying to watch, but it's the best way to improve.
    • Invite a client to co-present with you (as a nice value-add).
      ○ Most likely, you'll do 90% of the work.

❑ Use this speech as the foundation of a wide range of material you will reuse, repurpose, and republish, spreading it across the Internet. See the video at *https://goo.gl/gf9eHF*.
  ○ With a smartphone and a portable tripod with a phone clip, videotape your presentation.

- Upload the entire speech to Vimeo.com.
- Trim the speech into as many quality 2- to 3-minute snippets as possible, and upload each of them to YouTube as individual videos, once every couple weeks.
  - Use narrow, detailed keywords and buzzwords in the captions, tags, and descriptions so Google will index them thoroughly.
- Upload the PowerPoint slides to slideshare.net.
  - Create a thorough, detailed SlideShare profile.
  - Google highly ranks SlideShare profiles in name searches.
    - Connect the SlideShare slides to your LinkedIn profile.
- Post links and updates of your videos and slides to LinkedIn, Twitter, Facebook, and other social media accounts.
- If you're committed to speaking, hire an editor to turn your speeches into a demo video.
- For example, my speaker video is online at *www.youtube.com/watch?v=G1Abh_uo6LE.*

❑ Collaborate with your firm's Knowledge-Management, Marketing, and Business-Development professionals.

Knowing the difference between Marketing and Business Development is key. Marketing is focused on building your reputation and creating opportunities to get business. Business Development is building relationships and bringing in the business—the traditional Sales or Rainmaker activities. You'll need to do both at this stage in your career.

❑ Learn how to produce and leverage client information and competitive intelligence.
  - Use your firm library as a resource to help access competitive-intelligence information. There's an abundance of valuable information available.
  - Smart attorneys and firms understand how to leverage the power of critical information to create or identify demand.

❑ Continue adding to your social network with friends and close professional contacts.

❑ Continue to engage in at least one face-to-face marketing effort per week, such as breakfast, lunch, dinner, drinks, sports, social event, seminar, conference, or association meeting.

❑ Consider hiring a professional presentation consultant.

❑ Offer to host a meeting at the firm for a group in which you're active.

❑ Volunteer to help organize or host your law school's fifth-year reunion.
  ○ It's a great way to stay visible with hundreds of referral sources nationwide.
  ○ Repeat for future reunions.

Sixth Plus-Year Associates

MINDSET:

Start demonstrating that you're ready for partnership.

Stay in touch with and provide value to clients.

Share successes with contacts.

Enhance external profile and increase visibility.

❏ Work with a practice-group leader or mentor to set annual business-development goals.

❏ Continue the activities listed above, supplemented with additional activities:

❏ Meet with contacts at other professional-services firms (accounting, financial services, real estate, management consulting, public relations, practice-area boutiques) to identify strategic-partnership opportunities such as co-hosted events, client teams, and referrals.
  ○ Follow-up to events and meetings is critical.

❏ Unless your practice area is driven primarily through lawyer referrals (e.g., litigation boutique, appellate, personal injury, divorce, patent, admiralty), reduce your bar association activities and instead surround yourself with business prospects, rather than competitors.

❏ Work toward a leadership position in your selected industry association.
  ○ Consider running half-page ads in the industry publication, if
    • You would be the only law firm advertising there, and
    • You can make the ads visually interesting enough to truly stand out. See *https://youtu.be/jqy-x8GiE1E*.

❏ Co-author articles with clients in their industry publications.

❏ Co-present onstage or on a panel with clients at their industry events.

❏ Use technology to help grow and stay in touch with your network, e.g., blogs, Twitter, LinkedIn, etc.
  ○ Keep your platform narrow and focused. The world doesn't need another general "Real Estate" blog or Twitter feed.

❏ Request LinkedIn Recommendations, as appropriate.
  ○ Write Recommendations for clients and prospects. They'll appreciate it.

❏ Engage in at least two face-to-face marketing efforts per week.

❏ Ask your partners and business-development professionals to allow you to join them on pitches and client-assessment visits when appropriate.

❑ Ask your clients if they would like your help in reviewing their strategic plans, incoming Requests for Proposals, and outgoing proposals.

❑ If your small firm is already paying for Lawyers.com or and Martindale.com listings, seek both Peer and Client Ratings/ Reviews. *(http://research.lawyers.com/lawyer-ratings.html)*

Networking and Attending Seminars

- ❏ Networking is a long-term process. Learn to meet more of the right people, those whom you can turn into prospects, business contacts, then clients.
  - ○ "Active listening" is important.
  - ○ Ask well-informed questions regarding their business.
  - ○ Listen for opportunities and ways to help them achieve their goals.
  - ○ Ask your firm to bring in training on networking skills (See my brief video at https://goo.gl/Bwq9ii).
    - Networking is a learned skill. It's not difficult, but many behaviors seem counter-intuitive.
    - Most importantly, remember that the best information is gleaned by listening, not talking.

- ❏ Before the Event
  - ○ Determine whether the event you'll be attending is business or social.
    - If it's social, great, have fun. But if it's business, then you'll need to be more intentional and strategic, and invariably have less fun.
  - ○ When blocking off the event on your calendar, block off an additional hour in addition to the scheduled time.
    - Commit to arriving 30 minutes before the program starts and staying 30 minutes later—that's when the actual networking occurs, not during the presentation.
    - If your goal is to create new relationships or reinforce existing ones, this extra networking time is important.
  - ○ Consider doing some quick Internet research regarding any targets or prospects whom you expect to be at the event.
    - This information gives you an easy conversation starter ("Hey, I read that you were [doing X]. Tell me about that!")
    - It also positions you as the type of informed, educated professional they should want to work with.
  - ○ Write down a few simple, tangible goals to complete. They can be simple, e.g. "Meet two new people," or "Collect three business cards," or "Speak with Amanda at ABC Company."
    - Identifying specific goals makes your behavior more strategic and intentional; it'll guide your movements and let you know if you've been successful.

- One goal should be to speak with an existing contact you know will be there.
  - Ask two questions: "How's business?" and "What are you working on that you find especially interesting?"
- *Helpful hint:* Carry small "thank you" cards in your purse for quick, efficient follow-up.

❑ *During* the Event
  - Be strategic regarding whom you speak to. You're busy and you have taken valuable billable time away from work to be here.
  - You have only 30 minutes to meet and speak with the people you need to help advance your career. You can't afford to risk spending this time with the "wrong" people.
  - Subtly read their name tag and assess whether they fit your strategic profile *before* approaching and engaging them in conversation. (Don't get caught doing it.)
    - It might feel a tad mercenary, but remember, you've decided that this is *business*. You're at this event to meet new people who might turn into prospects and clients, not to make friends. That's for some other time or event.
  - Don't sit at empty tables. The same rule applies to where you sit—be deliberate regarding whom you'll spend lunch with.
    - Choose your seatmates carefully, intentionally, and subtly.
    - You'll spend an important hour between these two people. Make sure they're the "right" people for this occasion.
  - Try to meet more, rather than fewer people.

❑ Wear a name tag
  - If you need to write your own, make it neat, large, and legible. It helps attendees ask you questions and remember you later.
  - Affix name tags to your *right* lapel, not your left. This way it faces towards people when shaking hands with them.
  - You may need to plan ahead regarding your fashion choices to avoid damaging fragile clothing with a name tag's sticker or clip.
    - Have a selection of indestructible "conference blazers."
    - Keep one hanging on your door at work for last-minute programs.
  - If you're given a lanyard, position it above your chest so people can comfortably see it.
    - It may have a spring-clip to resize it. Tie a knot if necessary.
    - A name tag dangling around your stomach is entirely invisible. These days, no one will risk being caught looking down there.

- ○ When you next receive a magnetic-clip name tag, consider keeping it in your briefcase. They're the most flexible and least destructive style and can be reused in future events.

- ❑ Networking Questions. It can be difficult to get started in conversation with a stranger. Try some of these.
  - ○ [Look at their name tag.] Tell me about [company].
    - • What do you do there?
    - • What kinds of products/services do you provide?
    - • Who are your target customers?
  - ○ How did you get started in _____?
  - ○ What do you enjoy most about what you do/the topic of the event?
  - ○ What changes are happening in your industry?
  - ○ What are some of the projects you are currently working on?
  - ○ What can I do to help you/your business?
  - ○ Would you teach me more about _____ [business/topic they have an interest in]?

- ❑ Graceful Exit. Once you've made a good impression with someone within your target audience, create a relevant follow-up meeting or activity, commit to that follow-up, then exit the conversation so you both can continue networking.
  - ○ It's socially acceptable to suggest that you need to make a call, use the restroom, say hello to someone you see across the room, or get a drink.
    - • A friend of mine always orders a half-glass of beer at the bar. This way, he's never more than a few ounces away from an excuse to get out of an unhelpful conversation.
  - ○ "I don't want to take up all your time. "I'd like to continue our conversation, so how about we plan to get together? "I'll email you in the next couple days."
    - • Then be sure that you *do* it.
      - ○ Write your promise on the back of their business card after you split up, so you'll remember.
      - ○ Don't get caught doing it, some people and cultures believe that writing on their business card is insulting.
    - • Follow-up is hard. But it works.
  - ○ Don't monopolize their networking; they want to speak with more people too.
    - • You must *force* yourself to keep moving. It's too easy to simply continue a positive conversation when things are going well.

- Fight the urge to speak only to your friends. Hanging out with them is easy and fun, but that's not why you're at this event.

❑ *After* the Event
  - ○ Connect with them on LinkedIn within 24 hours, with a brief personal note that reminds them of who you are.
  - ○ Use the information on the business cards to add them to your firm's contact list or database for appropriate mailings, holiday cards, etc.
  - ○ Try to send a follow-up email by the next afternoon. Keep it simple and to the point, such as, "Nice meeting you, let's continue our conversation over lunch."
    - Offer a specific date, time and place in your email. Don't waste time with endless noncommittal back-and-forth communications.
    - Be polite and assertive; they will appreciate your being direct.
  - ○ Follow up as promised. For example, you might say, "After we spoke, I looked into [the topic in question] that relates to our conversation. I have attached a couple of the firm's electronic updates on this issue. Are you signed up to receive them?"

❑ While it's important to provide the client with as much meaningful information as you can, it's also important to find out as much as possible about their business and role.

❑ Clients particularly value lawyers who understand their business and industry. Speaking the client's language can set you apart in a positive way.

❑ Think about a strategy for the specific kinds of business initiatives and legal work on which you would like to partner with clients.

Conduct a "Needs Assessment."

The basis for conducting this assessment is to identify the client's needs and objectives. It will also give you and the client the opportunity to work together to brainstorm and create a clear plan for the future.

The key is to strategize and present this information in a way that identify their questions and concerns and helps them achieve their future goals. If there are legal solutions to their concerns, you have a path to find a way to work together on them.

❑ Here are some powerful questions that show respect for the client, giving them an opportunity to share what's most important to them:
  ○ From your perspective, what would be a valuable way for us to spend this time together?
  ○ What would be useful for you to know about our firm?
  ○ What prompted your interest in our meeting?
  ○ In talking to some of our clients in your industry, I'm struck by a couple of particular issues they are grappling with. These include: [give examples]. How would these resonate with you and your management?
  ○ How is your organization reacting to... (a recent, important development in this client's industry or function)?
  ○ How are you handling... (new competition, cheap imports, a new regulatory framework)?
  ○ Is there is a particular competitor you admire?
  ○ Can you tell me what your biggest priorities are for this year?
  ○ What are your most significant opportunities for growth over the next several years?
  ○ What exactly do you mean when you say ["risk-averse," "dysfunctional," "challenging?"]
  ○ Who would you say are your most valuable customers?
  ○ What would your best customers say are the main reasons they do business with you?
  ○ Why do customers stay with you?
  ○ Why do customers leave?
  ○ When customers complain, what do they say?
  ○ How have your customers' expectations changed over the past five years?

- ○ How would you describe the biggest challenges facing your own customers?
- ○ What's the driving force behind this particular initiative? What is behind the drive to reduce costs, design a new organization, etc.?
- ○ What would "better" (risk management, organizational effectiveness, etc.) look like?
- ○ How much internal agreement is there about the problem and the possible solutions?
- ○ From your perspective, given everything we've discussed, what would be a helpful follow-up to this meeting?

❑ Any one of these can help you to show respect, gain trust, build rapport, and, ultimately, be likable.
- ○ Since people want to work with people they like, why not try *active listening*, rather than talking?

❑ Visit clients on-site at their offices, stores, factories, or facilities, at no charge.
- ○ Many rainmakers consider client visits to be the single most-important, most-effective marketing tool available.
- ○ Dress appropriately for the location (suit vs. jeans and work boots).
- ○ Tour the plant, meet employees.
- ○ Prepare for this visit. Research the client before you go, understand what your firm is doing for them holistically as well as what other firms they might be using for things like litigation or transactions.
  - Ask insightful, educated, well-researched questions.
  - Become more familiar with their industry's legal and business issues.
- ○ This is critical: You are there to enhance your relationship and learn how to represent them better. DO NOT SELL.

❑ Help arrange or lead Marketing and Business Development training of your younger associates.

❑ If you enjoy Twitter, follow the journalists who cover your practice area or industry.
- ○ Engage with them occasionally.
- ○ Build relationships with journalists who may ask you to act as a resource for articles.
- ○ Offer to provide expert commentary on cases or current legal developments.

- o Others who follow those journalists may follow you too.
  - Twitter is a geometric, not linear, platform.

❏ Talk to your marketing professionals regarding the analytics from your client alerts and blog posts and how you can use the information for business-development purposes.

❏ Write multiple versions of your elevator pitch.
  - o Quick version: One or two sentences
  - o Medium version: One to two paragraphs; an expansion of your quick version
  - o Long version: An expansion of your medium version; can include example clients, representative engagements, and other relevant information
  - o Alternative versions: Create customized versions of your elevator pitch for different audiences

General Mindset

Clients can't often tell whether you're doing a good technical job, but they can tell how well you're treating them.

Communicate regularly. Meet your obligations and deadlines. Be responsive—don't make clients wait to hear from you; try to return every call within two hours, and never let a call or email go unreturned overnight.

Treat every person at the firm with the utmost respect regardless of their gender, race, religion, sexual orientation, age, or title. Learn the names of all of the receptionists, administrative assistants, clerks, and messengers. It's not only the decent thing to do, people notice. It matters.

Always remember, whatever your job, always do more than is expected. Show that you care, that you take this important profession seriously and are dedicated to doing your best for the firm and its clients.

And understand that law can be a difficult and stressful career. We work long hours on intellectually and emotionally challenging projects for clients who may seem demanding and unappreciative. It is essential to take care of yourself. Eat right, get enough sleep and exercise, and spend time with your friends, family, and hobbies. Volunteer for a charity. Ensure you have a vibrant and fulfilling life outside of your practice as well.

Gender-Based Communication Musings

Susan here:

Women remain underrepresented at every level in corporate America, despite having earned more college degrees than men for over thirty years. Most organizations understand the need to do more—corporate commitment to gender diversity is at an all-time high. Nonetheless, progress remains slow—and may even be stalling.

One of the most-powerful explanations is the simplest—we have blind spots when it comes to diversity, and we can't solve problems we don't see or understand. Raise awareness in your own firm and lead by example. Women need to have an equal shot at the career-stretching assignments. To create equity in the workplace, we must help women and men communicate more effectively.

- Diversity and inclusivity are not the same things.
- Firms that are diverse and inclusive perform better than firms that are not.
- Diversity requires including women and men of different ages and races.
- Inclusivity calls for complete integration of all employees into all firm operations.
- Women and minorities benefit from having people who coach them on "political navigation" as well as skills development.

In the workplace, people are continuously—and often unconsciously—assessing your communication style for two sets of qualities: warmth (empathy, likeability, caring) and authority (power, credibility, status). In all cases, a communication style turns into a weakness when overdone. A female's collaborative approach can appear submissive and a male's directness can seem callous.

Men appear aggressive when their expansive postures infringe on other's personal space (sometimes called "manspreading"), when they have a "death grip" handshake, and when they emphasize status cues to the point where they look haughty and uncaring. Women are viewed as weak or passive when they are unnecessarily apologetic, when they smile excessively or inappropriately, and when they discount their own ideas and achievements.

Typically, women have the edge in collaborative environments where listening skills, inclusive of body language and empathy are highly valued, and are judged as better at dialogue. Women are more empathetic and less combative. Because they are better at listening, they can more effectively and consistently find client-centered solutions.

Without as much ego or bluster, they can find unique solutions to litigation, rather than just filing a lawsuit. Most clients want to avoid costly litigation, yet many male attorneys do not even consider seeking a creative solution or alternative. The client's real goal is to resolve the dispute and get back to making money. In this regard, a female attorney's inclination to listen and predisposition to be creative, offers a solid advantage.

Women are generally more patient and better listeners, positioning them to understand the client's real needs when negotiating a deal or trying to solve a client's business problem.

Research shows that success and likeability are positively correlated for men and negatively correlated for women. That is, when a man is successful, his peers often like him more; when a woman is successful, both men and women may like her less. This trade-off between success and likeability creates a double-bind for women. If a woman is competent, she does not seem nice enough, but if a woman seems really nice, she is considered less competent. This can constrain a woman's career advancement.

This bias often surfaces in the way women are described, both in passing and in performance reviews. When a woman asserts herself—for example, by speaking in a direct style or promoting her ideas—she is often called "aggressive" and "ambitious." Or worse. When a man does the same, he is considered "confident" and "strong."

According to Carol Goman, author of *The Silent Language of Leaders,* women display more "warm" body language cues. They are more likely to focus on those who are speaking by orienting head and torso to face participants. They lean forward, smile, synchronize their movements with others, nod and tilt their heads (the universal signal of listening, literally "giving someone your ear").

These are powerful and positive communication traits. Understanding these differences in gender-based communication give you an advantage. Use what you now know to grow and protect your practices, your client's company, and yourself.

The receiver makes meaning of the message—regardless of the sender's intent. Effective communication takes place when the sender confirms the message is received as the sender intended. For each person certain communication strategies are more effective than others. As men and women communicate differently, there are common practices that make building and maintaining relationships a bit easier. We suggest giving the following recommendations an old college try:

- Adapt to sudden changes in direction whether in your personal or professional life.
- Use an easy-going and, where appropriate, fun, approach to building and nurturing relationships with colleagues and clients.
- Be prepared to share problems openly with trusted advisors or mentors inside the firm.
- Provide information that stimulates conversation among people of differing personalities, views, and styles.
- Ask for others' thoughts and ideas—even if they conflict with your own.
- Don't always expect brief, specific answers, especially outside of the courtroom.
- Allow for storytelling—your own and that of others—in your life.
- Acknowledge unique talents and leadership skills, even when you are not the leader.
- Be clear on your expectations, desired outcomes and completion details.
- Support others' needs for new ideas, state-of-the-art technology, modern-day materials, and intellectual growth challenges.
- Offer others praise and appreciation when due, early and often.
- Indulge in occasional speculation, knowing sometimes the questions are more meaningful than the answers anyway.

Remember to engage in The Three R's: Reputation (marketing), Relationships (business development), and Responsiveness (client service), and you'll shine!

Assert yourself, even at the risk of conflict.

Stop playing small. Be assertive, not aggressive; be confident, not cocky. Listen with empathy, not judgment. Know that in this context, "no" usually means, "No, not right now." There are counterproductive behaviors in which women engage that must stop such as:

1. You wait to be asked. If you wait to be asked, the opportunity may never come. Be proactive and make the ask!

2. Criticism crushes you. Nobody's perfect, and not everyone is not going to show you the respect you deserve. you. But that doesn't diminish your success or your talent. Use criticism to make yourself better where it's valid. Ignore it when you sense jealousy.

3. Nobody knows what you do. Own it! Tell everyone what you do. They may need or want your help. If you believe in yourself and your skills, if you truly believe that you're the best choice to help them achieve their goals, then do not be modest about helping them see that.

The Struggle Is Real for Women in the Workplace

Many women pepper their suggestions with humble disclaimers. Speaking at a low volume, they speed through their ideas to save others' valuable time. If interrupted, women often wait to continue—men do not. If met with groundless opposition, women compromise or retreat altogether—men do not.

Female professionals often speak tentatively to soften any emotional blow in the message they're delivering. Men may see this as a sign of insecurity or, worse, incompetence. This hesitant style includes "upspeak," i.e. ending statements as if they are questions, and using hedging phrases such as "I'm not sure but…." Choose to communicate with confidence. If you don't believe what you're saying, why should anyone else?

Women also tend to favor proactive but unobtrusive methods to preventing obstacles. This is a laudable goal but working behind the scenes can mean not getting the credit for heading off what might have become a problem. Men, on the other hand, often favor the "white knight" approach that allows problems to erupt and gives them an opportunity to "save the day."

Early studies show women mimicked men in order to succeed. When women fail to promote their achievements, supervisors may overlook them. Women are judged on past performance and men are judged on opinions about their future potential.

Women's mistakes tend to be noticed more and remembered longer. Worse, their successes tend to be attributed to luck—or getting help from others, while men's are attributed to skill. When confronting gender bias, form a posse of men and women. Organize a group of supportive coworkers who will celebrate one another's successes. You'll all benefit from this arrangement: promoting your coworkers is good for their careers and elevates your own status.

Conclusion

Good communication is even more important in a firm that is diverse. With a mix of genders, races, nationalities or faiths, it's easy for people to accidentally offend each other. Listening more than you talk and doing so with empathy and not judgment helps you to understand life from another person's perspective. This will help you to enjoy deeply rewarding relationships with your colleagues and clients.

Effective communication will afford you the tools you need to attract new business, retain the clients you have, and expand on existing client relationships through cross-selling. Know your strengths and weaknesses. Be open, honest, and direct and never be afraid to speak out when you have something meaningful to say. Effective communication can resolve problems or, better yet, prevent them from developing in the first place.

If you follow this checklist, over time you should find that you have developed a significant network of contacts you can turn into clients. Moreover, you will have laid the foundation for a successful career, one that is fulfilling personally, professionally, and financially.

Your goal is to identify what you love to do, find a way to bring that into your practice. If you do, you may spend your time until retirement leaping out of bed every morning absolutely passionate about your personal life, your profession, your mental health, and your success—however you define it!

Our goal is to create equity in the law firm by helping women communicate effectively with the world—and men communicate with women!

Good luck and let us know if we can help!

Addendum

NICHE AND INDUSTRY MARKETING CHECKLIST: LONG VERSION

Niche/Industry Marketing© Worksheet for Lawyers

What industry or niche specialty practice should you focus on?

Target companies must be appropriate to the size of the firm:

- What's your specialty niche?

- What type work do you want more of?

- Are there people/industries you particularly enjoy?

- What types of companies are most likely to hire you?

What skills, interest, or passion leads to an appropriate target?

- Something interesting/unusual about you?

- Previous job/career providing insight?

- Family business you worked in?

- Spouse's business you have contact in?

- Existing client providing industry experience?

- Previous big win/case study to get you started?

- Personal connections to give you a leg up?

- A hobby that engenders useful insight?

Select *one* industry group or trade association.

Browse through the *Encyclopedia of Associations (see page 47)* and select a little-known, niche-oriented trade or professional association upon which to focus your marketing efforts—ideally a national organization with a nearby local chapter where you can focus your monthly networking activities. Surround yourself with *clients*, not competitors.

- You must be active, visible.

- Attend monthly meetings.

- Join the membership committee.

- Work to leadership position.
    - o Committee chair
    - o Conference chair

- Focus most of your marketing activities on this group.
    - o Networking, research, biography, articles, speeches, public relations, ads, etc.

Some ways to focus your practice, a health care example:

- **Geography:** "National" is usually too broad. Define a narrower geographic region.

- **Size of business:** Focus on a certain segment of the business (e.g. just small or large hospitals).

- **Type of business:** Subset of a larger industry (e.g. ambulatory care facilities).

- **Injury type:** Focus on a certain type of injury (e.g. punitive damages or emotional distress).

- **Practice area:** Specialize in a narrow area (e.g. kidney dialysis or anesthesiology).

- **Or a combination:** Select two among the list (e.g. radiology cases in small hospitals).

What do I do after identifying some likely organizations?

- Contact them; the information is in the *Encyclopedia of Associations*.

  "I represent companies in your industry and would like to learn more about your association. Do you have a local chapter?"

- Request membership information.

- Learn about pricing, benefits, member demographics. Are they your target prospects?

- Analyze the conference schedule, magazines, and website.

What's the plan?

- "We don't accept [vendor] members."

  "I can help members avoid trouble, protect them-selves, save money...

- Write articles for magazine, newsletter

- Preventive-law monthly column

- Local/national conference speeches

- Network monthly at local meetings

- Advertise

Summary

Focusing your marketing clarifies your message and identifies how to use the standard tools most efficiently and effectively:

- Website
  - *Micro-site or blog* directly on point.

- Networking
  - *Finite audience* to meet.

- Research
  - *Specific industry* to learn about.

- Biography
  - *Tailored experience* to describe.

- Social media
  - *Add to LinkedIn bio.*
  - *Twitter* can establish expertise with the media.

- Brochure, print or electronic
  - *Targeted* to group's needs.

- Articles
  - *Focused message* is easy to discuss in print or on blogs.

- Speeches, Newsletters
  - *Interested audience* and a narrow topic.

- Public relations, quotes
  - *You're the expert,* so reporters need you.

- Advertising
  - *Inexpensive placement* in targeted publications or online.

NICHE/INDUSTRY MARKETING CHECKLIST: SHORT VERSION

Seek to identify one or more narrow niches in which, if effectively marketed, you could use to build a successful, focused practice. Where can you become a market leader? This form seeks to focus your thoughts regarding where to start.

Consider specific industries, narrow market segments, target communities, geographic regions, sub-practice specialties, and/or areas of narrow expertise. Avoid broad, traditional headings like Health Care, Real Estate, Insurance, Construction, or Financial Services. In what niche do you have the threshold level of expertise and limited law firm competition?

1. What narrow niche or industry should you consider targeting?

2. Identify any other firm lawyers who have experience in the target area.

3. Briefly describe your interest or expertise for this niche or industry.

4. Identify one or more existing clients or contacts in the targeted area.

5. Identify the best trade associations or similar organizations serving the target area, if you know (or look in Gale Publishing's *Encyclopedia of Associations*)

6. Identify any lawyers or firm(s) who would be your primary competitors.

7. How might you or the firm distinguish yourself from competing law firms in those areas?

INDIVIDUAL MARKETING PLAN: LONG VERSION

Describe Your Personal Marketing Goals for [year]

I. Developing Your Network and Reputation

Clients perceive professional activities like writing, speaking, and bar- and industry-association activities as indications of your knowledge and skill. Ensure clients know about your activities by sharing through the firm's marketing outreach, and posting to social media.

A. Networking

Networking is the foundation of client development. Build a network of the *right* contacts. After a thorough analysis, *precisely* identify the most likely sources of new business for the practice you are trying to develop—your "target audience." Next, find out which industry or trade associations they belong to and which meetings they attend. Then join those organizations and *work toward a leadership position.* You can't get business if the people who hand out the business don't know, trust, and respect you. This is a critical, *long-term* professional-development activity.

I will actively participate as a member of:

❑ **Industry or Trade Association(s)** In which *industry* would you like to develop contacts? What groups do your clients belong to?

❑ **Bar Association(s)** These help professional development and build a strong resume. For business-development purposes, it is better to be the only lawyer in a roomful of potential clients than sitting among other lawyers. Allocate your time carefully. As a young lawyer, select one bar association and work toward a leadership position. *Get active and visible!*

II. Developing Existing Client and Prospect Relationships

It is important to focus much of your marketing efforts on maintaining and expanding existing relationships.

A. Strengthening and Expanding Existing Client Relationships

Roughly 80% of a firm's new business comes from the top 20% of its clients. Lawyers should commit to strengthening, enhancing, and expanding these top relationships. The primary focus is to learn more about their businesses and industries, strategic business goals, and legal needs so that you can provide more informed and useful counsel. An added benefit of this enhanced understanding is that it positions you to identify new business opportunities. As the General Counsel of a Fortune 500 company said, "If you're not willing to take the time to learn about me, you do not really want my business." List the two current clients you will work to strengthen the firm's relationship with.

Existing Client's Name:

- ❏ **Company Research.** It is important to have current information about firm clients. To learn more about their company and industry so that I can serve them better, I will review their website, including the "What's New" section. I will leverage firm resources to learn more about my clients. (see *www.google.com/alerts*)

- ❏ **Client Visit (5th-year associates and up).** Within 6 weeks, I will volunteer to visit the client's facility, for free, to learn more about them and invest in the relationship, so that I can understand their business and enhance our service. I will tour the facility, and meet their people at all levels, but I will not market to them in any way. Instead I will learn about their goals, personnel, products, and operations.

❑ **Attend Trade Conference.** This year, I will offer to go with the client to his/her trade association conference at no charge, to learn more about his/her business and industry.

❑ **Read Industry Periodicals.** Within two weeks, I will view online and/or subscribe to (and read) the client's and competitor's trade journal(s) or blogs, to learn more about his/her business, industry, and jargon. The client would be delighted to learn of my interest and inform me of the best publications to read.

❑ **Write Industry Article.** This year, I will co-author an article or blog post with a client.

❑ **Make Conference Speech.** This year, I will arrange to speak at the association's next conference on a topic of particular relevance to this industry, co-presenting with a client if possible.

❑ **Attend Client Meetings.** This month and every two months thereafter, I will offer to attend the client's internal meetings, at no charge, to learn more about them, and offer advice on accomplishing its goals.

❑ **Entertain Client.** Every two months, I will entertain this client for a meal, event, etc.

❑ **Present In-House Seminar.** I will offer to conduct a free seminar on a useful topic.

❑ **Add to Mailing List.** I will ensure that this client and its key personnel are on our list.

B. New Client Development

Although it is a less-efficient way of bringing in new business, developing new clients is still important. List below one non-client target you will seek to develop business from during the coming year, and any additional support that you need to help you accomplish this.

Prospect's Name:

- ❑ I will conduct current company research.

- ❑ I will seek to visit the prospect's premises within six weeks.

- ❑ I will attend the prospect's industry/trade association meeting this year.

- ❑ I will view online and/or subscribe to (and read) the prospect's relevant trade journals and blogs within two weeks.

- ❑ I will co-author with a prospect a short, industry-focused article this year.

- ❑ I will seek to co-present with a prospect an industry association speech this year.

- ❑ I will volunteer every two months to attend the prospect's internal meetings.

- ❑ I will entertain this prospect every two months.

- ❑ I will seek to present an in-house seminar to this prospect.

- ❑ I will add this prospect to the mailing list.

III. Additional Resources

What would help you succeed with your marketing?
List the top 5 in order.

(1 is "least important" and 5 is "most important").

_____ Training in how to network or work a room better

_____ Training in how to focus my marketing to achieve better results

_____ Training in how to be more effective in new-business proposals and competitions

_____ Training in advanced client-service strategies

_____ More individual instruction/coaching

_____ Assistance from colleagues (describe:)

_____ Institutional support and leadership

_____ More knowledge of firm capabilities

_____ More time

Describe:

_____

_____

_____

_____

_____

_____

_____

III. Additional Resources

What would help you succeed with your marketing?
List the top 5 in order.

(1 is "least important" and 5 is "most important").

_____ Training in how to network or work a room better

_____ Training in how to focus my marketing to achieve better results

_____ Training in how to be more effective in new-business proposals and competitions

_____ Training in advanced client-service strategies

_____ More individual instruction/coaching

_____ Assistance from colleagues (describe:)

_____ Institutional support and leadership

_____ More knowledge of firm capabilities

_____ More time

Describe:

_____

_____

_____

_____

_____

_____

_____

INDIVIDUAL MARKETING PLAN: SHORT VERSION

MY 100-DAY INDIVIDUAL MARKETING PLAN

Clients: In the next 100 days, I will focus on increasing our involvement with the following existing clients (list clients and indicate the type of contact you will make with each client):

1. _____

_____

2. _____

_____

3. _____

_____

Prospects: In the next 100 days, I will initiate contact with the following organizations who are not currently clients of the Firm (list prospects and indicate the type of contact you will make):

1. _____

_____

2. _____

_____

3. _____

_____

Meetings: I anticipate having the following new-business meetings (face-to-face meetings with potential buyers) during the next 100 days (list):

Current Clients   **Prospects**

_____   _____

_____   _____

Positioning: In the next 100 days, I will conduct the following "positioning/broadcasting" business-development activities (speeches, articles, seminars, mailings—general passive marketing activities):

1. _____

_____

2. _____

_____

3. _____

_____

Proposals: I anticipate developing the following proposals for our services during the next 100 days (list):

1. _____

_____

2. _____

_____

Other: I will conduct the following "other" business development activities during the next 100 days:

Hours: I plan on devoting _____ hours per week to business development during the next 100 days.

Evaluation: The ways I will evaluate my business development efforts at the end of the 100 days will include: _____

HOW TO WRITE FOR THE INTERNET AND ENHANCE YOUR SEO

Biographies, LinkedIn pages, blog posts, and other online material can and should be used to elevate your rankings on search engines like Google (called Search-Engine Optimization, or SEO). We know roughly what Google's algorithms are looking for, which makes it possible to draft your materials in a way that uses this information to improve your results. Although there are no guarantees and the rules continue to change, leveraging this information and staying current on the trends and updates improves your chance of being found by your target audience of buyers and referral sources.

Fundamentally, Google tries to connect each search with the specific pages on credible websites that seem to best match that search. Therefore, when drafting the pages you would like ranked highly by Google, write from the perspective of a prospect seeking that information, working backwards from the specific Google searches they would conduct. Consider the exact terms they would use in the search box and use that same language in your online materials, like websites, LinkedIn, and other social media.

These days, sophisticated users are conducting longer, more complex searches, including narrow specialty areas or identifying particular types of contracts, clauses, phrases, or statutes. They include the name of the city, state, or province which means you should also if you want to persuade Google that your page is highly relevant.

Here is one of the least-known, but most-important pieces of information in this area: There are no "actual" Google search results—results differ on every computer. Google basically knows who and where you are, and tries to tailor the results to be most helpful to what you're probably looking for. This means that your search results will be very different from someone conducting the exact same search down the hall or in a different city or country. It's why when you search for "Plumber" you'll see plumbers in your local geographic area and not from Paris or São Paulo.

This reality can lead to biased results and a false confidence in your success. When you conduct a general "organic" search, your firm may receive a high ranking because Google knows your personal search history and your previous interest in that firm. But a more objective or disinterested searcher, like a prospect searching from a different city, might not find you on Google at all.

It's not unreasonable for sophisticated purchasers of legal services in the US to look for a skilled law firm in a far-flung jurisdiction by searching online. They might not do that for a major practice area in a major US city (e.g. "Boston litigation") where they can easily find a direct, in-person referral. But when seeking a professional in a smaller or less-well-known jurisdiction, Google searches become a useful option. But a firm buried on page 3 or lower will be out of competition. And that's a missed opportunity.

WRITING AN SEO-ENHANCED PRACTICE-AREA PAGE

- Describe the type of issues, services, questions, and tasks you deal with everyday.
- Engage your target audience by writing your text from your prospect's perspective. Let's consider an Intellectual Property group:
  - The firm may proudly offer a "full-service IP practice," but hot prospects rarely search for the terms "IP" or "intellectual property."
  - They more commonly seek "trade secret policy" or "registration of trade marks" or "licensing agreement." Therefore, those are the terms you should use in your practice pages as well.
- Refer to relevant statutes, landmark cases, seminal doctrine.
- Drop in the name of your firm instead of simply referring to "we."
- Include specific geography—the cities, states, provinces, and countries you serve.
- Mention that *"[Name of your firm] represents clients in the following counties:"*
  - List the counties or judicial subdivisions by name. Be careful, if the list is too long, Google may think that you're trying to inappropriately "pack" these terms, and penalize you.
- List the articles that you have written.
- If you are writing for your practice group, add: "Contact [name of attorney] at [phone number] or [email address] for more information regarding our [practice group] Law practice."
- List the names of the attorneys in the practice group, and link each name to their respective profiles.
- Add examples of work you may have done that validates the answer, e.g. client names, attorney names, cases won, and relevant statues.
- When referring to cases or statutes, you may add the complete title or link directly to them.

WRITING AN EFFECTIVE INDUSTRY-GROUP PAGE

Industry pages offer the opportunity to mix keywords that are difficult to impart in the text relating to your professional profile or practice area. This includes geographic terms (e.g. Detroit, Motor City, Michigan, Midwest), techno-legal terms (such as "molder's liens"), and statutory references (statutes, agencies, cases, and conferences).

Here is an example of a strong industry page prepared by a Detroit-based client:

CONTRACT AND SUPPLY CHAIN COUNSELING PAGE

With our roots in the Motor City and decades of combined experience, our contract and supply chain-counseling team at [Firm Name] understands the risks, costs, and challenges of the automotive and manufacturing supply chains. This in-depth knowledge enables us to provide some of the world's largest manufacturing clients with practical and detailed advice regarding how to understand, mitigate, and allocate the risks associated with selling complex automotive and non-automotive components, assemblies, and systems in a relentlessly competitive environment.

We help our clients with:
- Supply chain contracts and long-term agreements
- Terms and conditions of purchase and sale
- Pricing and material economics contracting, planning, and training
- Tooling and molder's liens and asset protection
- Supply chain risk/allocation gap analyses
- Warranty and warranty share agreements
- Intellectual property and trade secret agreements regarding manufacturing assets and know-how

Our team also helps automotive manufacturing companies understand and comply with the applicable safety and regulatory rules and regulations affecting their products, including:

- National Highway Traffic Safety Administration (NHTSA) rules, compliance and reporting
- Understanding and managing voluntary and mandatory recalls
- TREAD Act and Early-Warning Reporting planning and compliance
- Training, planning, and counseling for automotive manufacturers new to the United States

You will notice that any of the topics on this page could be live links that open to new pages that would speak to such topics in greater detail—you can start developing those pages when you have time.

Finally, one last word on the makeup of this page: you can also link certain of the items to other parts of the site. For instance, "TREAD Act" could link back to (i) a specific practice page; (ii) the profile of one of the attorneys who specializes on the application of this statute; or (iii) an event, conference, or article that speaks to this subject. These "lateral links" can create significant improvement both from an SEO and user-experience perspective.

Similarly, when drafting your profile, consider the references and links that can be made to specific industries.

WRITING A GREAT WEBSITE BIOGRAPHY/PROFILE PAGE

One of your most important marketing tools is a persuasive website biography. Most prospects will check out your bio before deciding whether to meet with or hire you. Website visitors are looking to identify an attorney with specific skills and experience, and match that against their particular needs.

Profile

While there are several ways to organize the content on a biography page, we suggest that you present the information as follows:

A. High-level summary

In 50 to 100 words, summarize your key skills. Refer to your position in the firm, reputation in legal circles, and standing in an industry. This is also where you can reinforce the main attributes of your firm's brand messaging with a personal message.

This short paragraph can also serve as your signature abstract that you would use whenever there is a reference to you outside the website (in a program where you are speaking, an article you wrote, a video where you are featured, etc.)

You may also list your most recent article, blog post, conference, or presentation—only one such entry is necessary here.

B. Career Highlights

In bullet-point form, list your top five highlights: this is where you are "packaging" yourself in terms that are relevant to your target clients and prospects. Where appropriate, link back to specific practice-area or industry pages on the site. In addition to your general experience, be sure to detail any particular expertise you have in the narrow specialties, niches, or industries you have selected as your marketing targets.

The career highlights should also be replicated in your LinkedIn profile.

This is also where you refer to your practice area(s), and responsibilities in such practice areas.

C. Particulars
- Education
- Publications: list articles, presentations, blogs, videos (with full title) and if possible an abstract of the subject dealt with in such material. All such material should be linked to the full version of the publication. Add a statement that you would be happy to send copies of the articles.
- Bar / Court Admittance
- Memberships
- Awards / Honors
- Social Platforms: addresses and links
- Community involvement with links to landing pages on the site for any association where you hold a leadership position. This is where you have a chance to articulate your commitment to such cause.

D. Complete resume
You can offer your visitor the opportunity to review or access a comprehensive listing of your resume. In such a listing, you should provide full descriptions of relevant matters, such as the complete name of tribunals where cases are heard, cited cases, deals, and press clippings.

Photo
Your headshot/photo should be recent and produced by a professional photographer.

Coordinates

The following basic information should also be made available:

- Name
- Office phone
- Cell phone
- Address (if multiple offices)
- vCard
- Name of assistant
- Practice area(s)
- Email
- LinkedIn profile link

DRAFTING A PERSUASIVE LINKEDIN PROFILE

This memorandum will serve as a checklist of essential items that should appear on your LinkedIn profile.

1. List Your Full Name

Do not use abbreviations. Married women who changed their name should include their maiden name as well.

2. Display a Professional Photo

There are reasons why some people don't want to display their photos, but this is a social networking platform. Not displaying your photo raises more questions than provides answers. Ensure that it is a professional, high-quality photograph. LinkedIn is not Facebook; do not use cropped group, vacation, or wedding photos. No props or artistic effects. Express your personality, but err on the side being more conservative. Here's the LinkedIn photo of Joe Fasi, whom I write about on pages 96-97. Doesn't he look solid and trustworthy? Don't you already want him as your lawyer?

3. Have a Professional Headline That Properly Brands You

In the space underneath your name is your "Professional" or Profile Headline. It will appear in search results next to your name, as well as next to any questions you ask or answer. It is, in essence, your elevator pitch in a few words. Do not simply put your title and firm name here: this is the place to interest anyone who finds you in a LinkedIn search result to learn more about you.

Think more in terms of "Raleigh Property Tax Attorney" or "North Carolina Family Law," rather than "Associate, Smith & Jones LLC."

4. Have Something Relevant and Timely in Your Status Update

The Status Update is about showing that you are still relevant in doing whatever you are doing. Going to an event? Share it. Attending a conference? Share it. Read something interesting that is relevant to your brand? Share it. Use your Status Update to show your relevance, and try to aim for a once-a-week update. You don't want someone visiting your profile and see a Status Update that is months old...

For those who enjoy writing, LinkedIn is an ideal platform to push out your articles.

5. Display Enough Work Experience... with Details

Your LinkedIn profile doesn't need to be a resume. One simple sentence summarizing what you did is enough to ensure that a potential reader understand the role that you had. Job descriptions provide you the perfect opportunity to pepper your profile with narrow, search engine-friendly keywords that will help you get found. For example:

Amber concentrates her practice in the area of litigation, with a primary emphasis on litigating large commercial disputes. She regularly represents financial institutions, corporations, limited liability companies and individuals in contract, corporate, shareholder, U.C.C. and fiduciary disputes in all of the federal and state courts of North Carolina, including the North Carolina Business Court.

6. List Your Education

Put education details on your profile. What did you achieve at a certain school? Honors, awards, or activities? Mention them.

7. Get Some Recommendations

The LinkedIn "profile completeness" algorithm requires that you receive three recommendations in order to get to 100%. This is not critical, but is useful. Do not be embarrassed to ask friends who know you well to recommend you; it's a well-understood part of social networking today. And when you've done something particularly great for a client, that's the optimal time to sheepishly tell them that "the firm's marketer insisted that we ask for some LinkedIn recommendation." That is, blame "Marketing" if it'll make you feel less awkward to ask; your client will understand. Email them the link, to make it easier for them. And of course, it's only polite to recommend them back!

8. Acquire Connections

If you're on LinkedIn you should be networking. Connections are also important to help get found in the huge LinkedIn database. Rule of thumb? Multiply your age by 10 and that is the *minimum* number of connections that you should have. Join some relevant practice and industry groups and connect with the members you know. Start with your firm, any previous firms you've worked for or jobs you've held, and your law school class. Connect, connect, connect.

9. Your Professional Summary is *Essential*

The Professional Summary section is the first thing people will read, right after your headline. Don't just dump the first 2,000 characters of your standard resume into your LinkedIn Summary. This is how you will introduce yourself to your professional contacts, and future clients, referral sources, and employers. This is the most-important professional social-networking platform, so why not spend a few minutes introducing yourself? This is the place for you to tell your own story, in your own voice, typically with a bit more personality than your firm's website bio.

Devote the time necessary to make your Summary truly great. Admittedly it can be difficult to write this way about yourself, so get some help if necessary from a professional writer, or perhaps an old friend who aced that college creative writing class.

Here's a LinkedIn profile that I wrote for my friend Joe Fasi, one of the nation's top trial lawyers. Joe's a kind, modest guy, and he wins complex ten-figure cases because juries like and trust him. It's just 333 words long, but see if it helps you start forming a generally positive impression of him and his technical skills:

> Most people know the movie "The Maltese Falcon." I am not the Maltese Falcon, but I am from the island of Malta and speak fluent Maltese. I also like to speak to jurors, and do so often and in cases with large damages at stake. I've tried over 100 jury trials to verdict, defending complex cases with enormous exposure against sympathetic plaintiffs.
>
> I haven't counted up my precise win-loss record, but a client recently asked me "how the heck I keep winning all these cases." I wasn't exactly sure how to respond to that, but I smiled and thanked him for what he intended as a compliment. Thinking about it later, I suspect the answer might partly be that I don't get involved in the games that many litigators like to play. I don't play puerile hide-the-ball tricks. I'm aggressive, but honest and reasonable. I want a fair and just resolution and, if a plaintiff wants my client to pay a lot of money, they better prove that they're darn well entitled to every penny of it.
>
> In post-trial research, juries have universally said that they liked me—they felt I approached the trial with decency and integrity, and trusted me to help them get at the truth. This is particularly important because it means I become the face of the faceless corporation. I've helped level the playing field.
>
> Fewer and fewer large cases actually go to trial. When they do, I defend them, nationwide, for companies that are among

the most skilled and strategic purchasers of legal services, including manufacturers, pharmaceutical, and tobacco.

I typically handle cases as the lead trial attorney, getting hired at the outset to resolve a problematic dispute or lawsuit. Some companies use me as a their "go-to attorney," parachuting me in on the courthouse steps, either to support an existing trial team, or simply take over and handle the trial, especially the large or challenging cases.

Specialties: Product Liability, defense of nursing homes, and professional/medical liability.

11. Claim Your Personal URL

When you sign up to LinkedIn you are provided a complex "Public URL." You can customize and simplify this when you edit your profile with a couple simple steps. If you have a common name, make sure you claim your URL before others do! My LinkedIn URL is *https://www.linkedin.com/in/rossfishman/*. It's simple, and yours should be too. You can then include your abbreviated LinkedIn link on your email signature, business card, and everywhere else you go online. A quick Google search will find short videos detailing the simple steps.

12. Add Your Website(s).

You can add up to three website links. You will want to link to your blog and you may want to link to a page of any attorney directory where you're positively referenced. You should make a title for each website link — instead of having your firm name as the title, use something like "North Carolina Personal Property Tax Advisor."

13. Join Relevant Groups

You should join Groups that are relevant to your areas of interest and expertise, get active in the discussions to help meet people in your growing professional network, build your brand as a helpful and knowledgeable member of the community, and start connecting with the members as mentioned above.

HOW TO WRITE PERSUASIVE CASE STUDIES

Among the most persuasive components of a lawyer's written marketing arsenal is a current collection of case studies (also called "war stories"). Clients regularly comment that direct, relevant experience can be the decisive factor when selecting their attorneys for a particular case or matter. It is important to your marketing efforts to draft and maintain an updated collection of these examples as you go throughout your career.

In determining whom to hire, prospects are thinking, "Don't tell me that you *can* do something, show me that you've already *done* it successfully." This information is important to have in your online biographies, and for use in competitive new-business materials.

Attached is a simple, fill-in-the-blanks form to expedite the collection of this data. Before creating your own process, remember to leverage the professional staff at your firm to find out if there is additional information that you should collect or if there is firm-wide experience-management or knowledge-management system or process in place. You may choose to either fill in the blanks and start from there, or simply dictate the information following the Sample Summary format in the example shown below. With a little practice, you can dictate new case studies in just a minute or two.

LITIGATION CASE SUMMARY FORM

Case Facts:

1. The simple case caption was: _____
   _____
   _____

2. Client name: _____
   ❑ Plaintiff   ❑ Defendant

3. The court/jurisdiction was: _____
   _____
   _____

4. The *total* amount at issue was: $ _____

5. Client description - revenues, industry, etc. [e.g. $250 million
   pharmaceutical co.]: _____
   _____

6. Relevant issues/allegations of complaint:
   [e.g. fraud, RICO, breach of contract]:   _____
   _____
   _____

7. The names of the firm's legal team: _____
   _____
   _____

8. Full description of outcome (settlement, dismissal, jury verdict
   etc.): _____
   _____
   _____

Case Highlights:

9. IMPORTANT: Describe how the client benefited specifically by your work (e.g. how did you save them time or money, develop an innovative strategy or tactic, etc. that another lawyer might not have considered):

_____

_____

_____

_____

_____

_____

Sample Litigation Summary

This is a short, easy-to-read format that provides all the necessary "who, what, where, when, why, and how" information for your prospects. Remember to use plain English and short sentences, simplifying it as much as possible, targeting an eighth-grade reading level. It's not that your targets can't comprehend big words and complex sentences, just that when reading text online, they prefer not to.

Par-D, Inc. vs. U.R. Safe Company

We defended U.R. Safe, a middle-market manufacturer of smoke detectors, in a $5 million product liability, fraud, and wrongful death action in Vermont state court. The plaintiff alleged that a defective smoke detector manufactured by our client caused the fire which destroyed the plaintiff's liquor store. Following a month-long trial the jury returned a verdict in our client's favor on all counts in just 45 minutes. The case was settled on appeal, setting an important precedent in the field of liquor store conflagrations.

TRANSACTIONAL CASE SUMMARY FORM

Deal Facts:

1. Client name: _____

   _____

2. Other parties involved: _____

   _____

3. The *type* of transaction was: _____

   _____

4. The *total* amount of the deal was: $ _____

5. Client description - revenues, industry, etc.
   [*e.g.* $250 million pharmaceutical co.]: _____

   _____

   _____

6. The names of your legal team:

   _____

   _____

7. Description of the deal:

   _____

   _____

   _____

Deal Highlights:

9. IMPORTANT: Describe how the client benefited specifically by use of our firm (e.g. how did we save them time or money, develop an innovative structure, *etc.* that another firm might not have done):

_____

_____

_____

_____

10. May we use the name of this client in our marketing materials?
    ❏ Yes   ❏ No

Sample Deal Summary

This is a short, easy-to-read format that provides all the necessary "who, what, where, when, why, and how" information for your prospects. Remember to use plain English and short sentences, simplifying it as much as possible, targeting an eighth-grade reading level. It's not that your targets can't comprehend big words and complex sentences, just that when reading text online, they prefer not to.

Acme Incorporated

We represented Acme, a $500 million mail-order company engaged in the manufacture of roadrunner-catching devices, in a coordinated series of sophisticated financings totaling $250 million. These include its public offering of $135 million of senior subordinated notes and $115 million of senior secured discount notes. Proceeds from the note offering and the term loans, along with proceeds from a prior private placement of common stock, will be used to design and construct a new jet-propulsion backpack to be marketed to desert coyotes.

NOTES

NOTES

NOTES

Ross Fishman, J.D.

Ross Fishman is one of the legal profession's most popular marketing and ethics CLE keynote speakers. Often characterized as both highly entertaining and educational, Ross's presentations draw on his experience as a litigator, marketing director, and marketing partner, inspiring lawyers at all levels.

A Fellow of both the College of Law Practice Management and the Litigation Counsel of America (LCA), Ross has branded 200 law firms worldwide on six continents and has written 300 bylined articles including seven monthly columns. Selected as a "Lawdragon 100 Leading Consultants and Strategists, he received the international Legal Marketing Association's (LMA) first peer-selected Lifetime Achievement award and was the first marketer inducted into the LMA's international Hall of Fame.

A particular highlight was when a grateful Louisville law firm client had the Governor commission Ross as a Kentucky Colonel. He's been quoted in the media hundreds of times, in publications including *The Wall Street Journal,* The New York Times, and NPR's "All Things Considered."

A member of the federal Trial Bar (N.D. Ill.), Ross received a B.A. in Speech Communications, *cum laude*, from the University of Illinois, and his J.D. from Emory University School of Law. Subscribe to his marketing blog at *fishmanmarketing.com/blog.*

Contact Ross directly to book him for your associate-training program, firm or partner retreat, or marketing-training or Ethics/CLE programs, at ross@fishmanmarketing.com.

Susan Freeman, M.A.

Susan's goal is to help women in business communicate effectively with the world–and to help men communicate effectively with women in business! Susan's training draws on her experiences as a sales executive in the financial services industry, her business development and leadership training in the legal industry, and her graduate-level studies in Communication.

Susan's passion for helping women succeed is long-standing. She co-founded "Women's Business Connection" in Massachusetts and "Girl Power" with over 6,000 followers. She has also taught, "Girls in Politics," a program created to introduce girls to politics, policy, and the branches of government. Her enthusiasm for the benefits of building meaningful relationships has made her a great connector. As such, she has over 15,000 followers on social media. Susan excels at building relationships and teaching others to do the same, to communicate effectively and bring in business.

Susan has worked with some of the world's most-prestigious law firms and financial services institutions. Susan has lived in Louisiana, Switzerland, Italy, Massachusetts, Hawaii, and now, California. Throughout her sojourns, she has developed a large, interconnected circle. Susan lives in the Bay Area with her husband, Mike Futrell, and their son, James.

Acknowledgments

The Ultimate Law Firm Associate's Marketing Checklist was initially based upon my experience and memories working as a fresh-faced litigator at a progressive firm that offered marketing training to associates. Years later, working as an in-house legal marketer, I drafted the first 4-page version of this checklist, to support the industrious associates who eagerly sought advice.

I truly appreciate the countless suggestions I've received over the years from lawyers, marketers, and administrators, many of which I adapted to enhance the quality of the material. And during each new iteration, I sought input from industry peers who selflessly volunteered their unique perspectives. In this new edition, I am grateful to the experienced marketing and business-development professionals whose expert insight helped inform our thoughts in this new version. Our sincere thanks go out to all of them.

A very special thanks to Michelle Benjamin, Fishman Marketing's extraordinary Creative Director, for her invaluable work on 20 years of Fishman Marketing branding projects, including designing this book. Our most sincere thanks as well to our diligent copy editor, Andrew Fishman.

Finally, I am grateful to Fishman Marketing's valued clients who have trusted me over the years to educate their esteemed attorneys on the marketing techniques presented in this book.

Made in the USA
San Bernardino, CA
16 June 2019